THE REDEEMED CHRISTIAN CHURCH OF GOD
NORTH AMERICA

RCCGNA
YOUTH LESSONS
2023/2024

the Zeal

Year Theme
FREEDOM

So if the Son sets you free,
you will be free indeed.
— John 8:36

THE ZEAL FOR TEENS | 2023/2024

***The Zeal*, Redeemed Christian Church of God Youth Sunday School Guide 2023/2024**

Copyright © 2023 the Redeemed Christian Church of God North America

ISBN: 978-1-60924-186-5

All rights reserved. With the exception of brief excerpts for review purposes, no portion of this book may be reproduced or transmitted in any form or by any means, electronic or mechanical including photocopying, recording or by any information storage retrieval system without the written permission of the Redeemed Christian Church of God north America. Unless otherwise indicated, scriptures are taken from the King James Version of the Bible.

Printed in the United States of America.

Published by:
The Redeemed Christian Church of God North America
515 Co Rd 1118, Greenville, TX 75401

Cover, Inner layout, printing by:
Triumph Publishing
Bronx, new York, 10469
www.triumphpublishing.net
718-652-7157

TEENS' ZEAL FOR 2023/2024

VISION & MISSION STATEMENT

The following are our vision and goals of the Redeemed Christian Church of God:

- To make heaven.
- To take as many people as possible with us.
- To have a member of R.C.C.G. in every family of all nations.
- To accomplish No. 1 above, holiness will be our lifestyle.
- To accomplish No. 2 and No. 3 above, we will plant churches within five minutes' walking distance in every city and town of developing countries and within five minutes' driving distance in every city and town of developed countries.

We will pursue these objectives until every nation in the world is reached for JESUS CHRIST OUR LORD.

THE ZEAL FOR TEENS | 2023/2024

2023/2024 – Edition

Published by:
The Redeemed Christian Church of God North America
515 Co Rd 1118, Greenville, TX 75401

Production Crew:
Moji Olagbegi
Bola Elegbe
Adewale Akinrinde
Tayo Osinubi
Mayowa Agboola

CONTACT US:
Email: rccgnayouth1@gmail.com
Website: http://youth.rccgna.org
TO ORDER:
CONTACT: Bola Elegbe
732-485-3222
Email:rccgnayouth1@gmail.com

TO ORDER: MAKE CHECK PAYABLE TO RCCG AND MAIL:
Bola Elegbe @ 38 Brookfield Drive, Jackson, NJ 08527

NOTE: Books are ten dollars per copy
FOR MORE INFORMATION, PLEASE EMAIL: rccgnayouth1@gmail.com

PASTOR (MRS) FADEL'S Message

Dear Youth reader,

Welcome to a New Year!

A year filled with great possibilities, abundant blessings, and the overwhelming favor of God in the name of Jesus!

As you move into the new year, I want you to know that Christ is ALIVE in you!

Simple illustration: one light bulb can illuminate an entire room that would otherwise be filled with darkness. However, it cannot create light on its own without being connected to a much more powerful source. Similarly, as a youth, you are called to be vessels of light to all around you to carry the light and power of the love of Jesus Christ wherever you go. Believe it or not, you do have the potential to radiate the transforming power of God to everyone around you. **Matthew 5:16** says, *"In the same way, let your light shine before others, that they may see your good deeds and glorify your Father in heaven."*

As you use the manual this year, may it reveal two messages:
First, the message of salvation, if you have not accepted Christ as your Savior, and secondly, how to live a life that reflects the transforming life of Christ where His direction will be your direction and His will, your will.

As you study this manual each week, questions to ask yourself are, what am I reflecting to the people around me? If people didn't know I was a Christian, would my actions reflect those of Christ?

My prayer is that you will see HOW Christ can be fully alive in you and show you WHAT things that do not reflect His faith, hope, and love. Now having read this, GO AND LIGHT UP YOUR WORLD!

Much love and God's blessings,
Pastor Manita Fadel
Director, RCCG America's Children and Youth Ministry

TEACHER'S CORNER

Things to consider for effective impact!
1) Have a good knowledge of the material,
2) Prayer and preparation are the most important, and
3) Apply the message to your own lives.

Biblical Teaching has a long-lasting impact on actions.

You should have questions that fall into EACH of the THREE of the following areas:

1. **To know** – What do you want them to understand more clearly?

2. **To feel** – How do you want the group to feel? Challenged? Loved? Secure? Excited?

3. **To do** – An appeal for action – What do you want them to specifically do as a result of this time? You motivate them to accomplish this goal through the CONCLUSION and application time.

Start using your effective introduction and the kinds of questions you ask to make them personally feel the truth as applied to them. A real, lasting change happens only when the heart is added to the thinking.

Never forget the place of the Holy Spirit!

From my heart!
Pastor Moji Olagbegi

RCCG, NORTH AMERICA

TABLE OF
CONTENTS
THEME: *Freedom*

LESSON 1:	SECURED	11
LESSON 2:	POWER TO LIVE OUR BEST LIFE	13
LESSON 3:	THE FEAR FACTOR	15
LESSON 4:	GOD IS THINKING ABOUT YOU!	17
LESSON 5:	REVIEW 1	20
LESSON 6:	DO YOU BELIEVE IN MIRACLES?	21
LESSON 7:	WARNING!	23
LESSON 8:	UNPACKING THE SLAP!	25
LESSON 9:	UKRAINE	27
LESSON 10:	SOCIETY, SELF & FAMILY!	29
LESSON 11:	FREEZE	33
LESSON 12:	FIRST INTERACTIVE SESSION & QUIZ 1	35
LESSON 13:	HONEST TALK	36
LESSON 14:	SENIOR SUNDAY	39
LESSON 15:	GOD, I WISH SOMEBODY WOULD'VE TOLD ME WHEN I WAS YOUNGER!	41
LESSON 16:	HOW TO BE BLESSED	44
LESSON 17:	KNOW YOUR TEACHERS!	47
LESSON 18:	REVIEW 2	49
LESSON 19:	ENGAGING WITH SCRIPTURE	50
LESSON 20:	DOUBTING THOMAS (ACTIVITY)	53
LESSON 21:	DON'T GIVE IN TO DISTRACTIONS!	56
LESSON 22:	DO YOU SEE YOURSELF AS GOD SEES YOU?	58
LESSON 23:	DISTINCTION BETWEEN MORALITY AND CHRISTIANITY	61
LESSON 24:	SECOND INTERACTIVE SESSION AND QUIZ 2	63

THE ZEAL FOR TEENS | 2023/2024

TABLE OF CONTENTS

LESSON 25:	CAN YOU GUESS?	64
LESSON 26:	REWIND IT!	66
LESSON 27:	JUSTIFICATION & SANCTIFICATION	69
LESSON 28	BAPTISM	71
LESSON 29	WHAT MAKES AN ENGAGING WITNESS?	73
LESSON 30	REVIEW 3	76
LESSON 31	TEN-YEAR PLAN	77
LESSON 32	BEHIND THE NAME (ACTIVITY)	80
LESSON 33	ONE THING!	83
LESSON 34	DON'T MISS OUT!	85
LESSON 35	WHO IS YOUR MENTOR?	87
LESSON 36	"IN CHRIST"	89
LESSON 37	TEAMWORK (ACTIVITY)	91
LESSON 38	THIRD INTERACTIVE SESSION AND QUIZ 3	94
LESSON 39	WHAT LOVE DOES?	95
LESSON 40	BEHAVIOUR MODIFICATION	97
LESSON 41	I'M FORGIVEN (ACTIVITY – KARAOKE SUNDAY)	100
LESSON 42	THE MYTH ABOUT FORGIVENESS	102
LESSON 43	GOD THE ETERNAL CREATOR (PART 1)	105
LESSON 44	GOD THE ETERNAL CREATOR (PART 2)	109
LESSON 45	REVIEW 4	112
LESSON 46	LIVING IN A CORRUPT AND UNFAIR WORLD	113
LESSON 47	TOUGH QUESTIONS (PART 1)	115
LESSON 48	TOUGH QUESTIONS (PART 2)	117
LESSON 49	JESUS CLAMS THE STORM	119
LESSON 50	BECKY'S CONVERSION STORY	121
LESSON 51	WORDS MATTER!	128
LESSON 52	TAKE A STAND!	133
LESSON 53	FOURTH INTERACTIVE SESSION & QUIZ 4	135

Left blank intentionally

LESSON 1
SECURE

MAIN POINT: No matter what happens in your life, God has guaranteed your future if you trust in Jesus.

INTRODUCTION
We live in uncertain times. I guess everyone does somehow. Do you ever worry about the future? A lot of people do. They are afraid of what might happen to them, their fortunes, or their families. They're afraid of what might happen in the world, in their country or community. Whenever you feel unsettled or insecure, Psalm 125 is a great place to go.

CLASS DISCUSSION
Read Proverbs 18:10
- How and where can we be safe?
- Do you too trust in an untested territory?
- Can you take God at His word? Read Psalm 16:8
- What steps should we take NOT to be in a compromised situation?
- With all the evil and unrest in the world; can we still trust God to keep us safe? Job 11:18
- Read Psalm 37: 1-7
- On a scale of 1 – 10; how would you grade your trust and security in the following relationships?
    - Mom, dad, friends, God, school teacher, youth leader, siblings, grandparents, and pastor.
    - What are the reasons for your grades?

TALK IT OVER: Why is it so important to trust God?
- Who can you depend on for safety?

BIBLE READING

Psalm 125

MEMORY VERSE

I know the Lord is always with me. I will not be shaken, for he is right beside me. Psalm 16:8

THE ZEAL FOR TEENS | 2023/2024

LESSON 1
SECURE

- Have you ever struggled to believe in God's goodness?
- What helped you overcome those concerns? Or why not?
- How does knowing that your future is secure change how you live today?

READ OUT LOUD
- Romans 8:28 – "And we know what all that happens to us is working for our good if we love God and are fitting into his plans." TLB Version
- Psalm 32:8 – God will lead you in the way you should go.
- Those that have learned to obey and follow the voice of God are never defeated or destroyed.
- Psalm 91:11 – He gives His angels charge over you and they are committed to protecting you from all evil.
- He surrounds you with godly friends and people who became a wall of protection to you, and by their counsel, you can make wise and safe decisions that ensure your protection.

CONCLUSION
So, running to God for safety and security or protection requires obedience, faith, and trust from you.

CLOSE IN PRAYER!!

TEACHER'S CORNER: Keep a box in your meeting space where students can drop prayer requests. Take time each week to empty the box and pray for each need.

WEEKLY QUIET TIME

DAY	BIBLE PASSAGE	SHARE YOUR DISCOVERIES BELOW
Monday	Psalm 23	
Tuesday	Psalm 1	
Wednesday	Psalm 91:1- 8	
Thursday	Psalm 91:9 -16	
Friday	1 Peter 1: 3-4	
Saturday	Psalm 124	

LESSON 2
POWER TO LIVE OUR BEST LIFE

 MAIN POINT: Receive God's power to help live your best life.

BIBLE READING

Isaiah 40 25-31

INTRODUCTION
Our strength and wisdom will eventually run out, but God's power has no end. God intends for us to live by the power and authority given to us. To do this, we must maintain a close relationship with God, both through prayer and by trusting His Word.

MEMORY VERSE

"He gives power to the tired and worn out, and strength to the weak."
Isaiah 40:29

CLASS DISCUSSION
READ Isaiah 40:31 & Matthew 8:23-34
Answer the following questions; please support your answers with Scriptures!
- What do we understand from the two Scriptures above?
- What is our role?
- Who or what else has power over you?
- How can you receive power from God?
- What can God's power not do?
- Do you need God's power?
- Where in the Bible does it say you shall receive power?

TALK IT OVER: *(Teachers, please discuss and give life examples)*
- How to use your spiritual authority in any situation
- Please explain Luke 10:19.
- How do you decide between the many voices directed at you? And learn to listen to God's Spirit?

LESSON 2
POWER TO LIVE THE BEST LIFE

CHEW ON IT: The words of Jesus are true and reliable, more so than anything else we could read or hear or imagine. His authority comes from the Lord. And where do we get His words? Bible!

CONCLUSION
Every force is subject to the power and authority of Jesus. We can, indeed, have faith that Jesus can do anything He wants to do in our lives. Just as Jesus delivered the men in the Decapolis from demons, He can deliver you from a physical, spiritual, emotional, psychological, or mental challenge. Have faith in the power and authority of Jesus.

CLOSE IN PRAYER!!

WEEKLY QUIET TIME

DAY	BIBLE PASSAGE	SHARE YOUR DISCOVERIES BELOW
Monday	Psalm 34: 8 – 13	
Tuesday	Psalm 34: 14 – 18	
Wednesday	Amos 5: 13 – 17	
Thursday	1 Peter 4: 7 – 12	
Friday	1 Peter 4: 13 – 19	
Saturday	1 John 3: 11-24	

LESSON 3
THE FEAR FACTOR

 MAIN POINT: Fear can make us focus more on what we're afraid of than what we are trying to accomplish. Satan uses fear to distract us from something God wants us to do. The Bible talks a lot about fear and gives us instructions on how to handle fear.

BIBLE READING

2 Timothy 1:7 (NLT)

MEMORY VERSE

"I prayed to the LORD, and he answered me. He freed me from all my fears." Psalm 34:4

INTRODUCTION
Everyone knows what it is like to be afraid. We all have things that we are afraid of – lightning, snakes, criminals, or the unknown. There are also hidden fears that affect us but through our faith in Jesus, we can learn to overcome moments of fear.

CLASS ACTIVITY
Instructions: Teachers, please let the students watch the first five minutes of the video using their phones; https://youtu.be/4G6t9OhO4M8

Fear Factor is a UK and American TV show that begins with an introduction from the narrator, and the phrase "Imagine a world where your greatest fears become reality" is the most used opening line!

CLASS DISCUSSION
The goal of our discussion is to learn how best we can overcome fear and live by faith. EVERYONE knows what it is like to be afraid. There are also hidden fears that affect us.

- Read Psalm 34:4 and share a time in which prayer made a difference in your life.
- Write the Scriptures down below in your own words:

LESSON 3
THE FEAR FACTOR

- 2 Timothy 1:7 _____
  _____
- Proverbs 29:25 _____
  _____
- Psalm 56:3 _____
  _____
- Explain what 1 John 4: 18-19 means.
- What 2 Timothy 1:7 saying to you?
- How can we handle fear of rejection?
- God has empowered us to live by the power of His Spirit to overcome fear and live a victorious life; how?

ACTION
- What did King David do to overcome his fears? Read Psalm 34; how can you use this in your life!
- Have faith in the word of God; **Isaiah 41:10**

CONCLUSION
Fear is nothing more than "False Evidence Appearing Real". We have two choices; forget everything and run or face everything and rise. If we do not face off with our fears, they will keep us from living the victorious life God has planned for us.

CLOSE IN PRAYER!!

WEEKLY QUIET TIME

DAY	BIBLE PASSAGE	SHARE YOUR DISCOVERIES BELOW
Monday	Psalm 46	
Tuesday	Deuteronomy 3:22	
Wednesday	Deuteronomy 31:8	
Thursday	Judges 6:23	
Friday	Psalm 27:3	
Saturday	Psalm 118:6	

LESSON 4
GOD IS THINKING ABOUT YOU!

 MAIN POINT: The Lord loves His people so much that He can't keep Himself from thinking about us. We are always on His mind.

BIBLE READING
Isaiah 55: 8-11

INTRODUCTION
I cannot have any fellowship with God if my thoughts and His thoughts are in opposite directions. My thoughts must be conformed to God's thoughts, if not, I cannot be like Him and walk with Him.

MEMORY VERSE
"How precious are your thoughts about me, O God. They cannot be numbered!" Psalm 139:17

CLASS ACTIVITY
Listen to the song "Friend of God" by Israel Houghton; feel free to sing along!
https://youtu.be/UI0cgUKMqRs

Lyrics
I am a friend of God
I am a friend of God
I am a friend of God He calls me friend
Who am I that You are mindful of me
That You hear me when I call
Is it true that You are thinking of me
How You love me it's amazing

Repeat
I am a friend of God
I am a friend of God
I am a friend of God
He calls me friend.

CLASS DISCUSSION
- What's your take on the song and the lyrics?
- Can you connect the song with John 15:14?

THE ZEAL FOR TEENS | 2023/2024

LESSON 4
GOD IS THINKING ABOUT YOU!

- Where and how do we know the thought of God?
- Why is God thinking about me?
- And what should my response be?
- Knowing God's thought towards us help us to _____
_____
- What comes to mind when you think about God? _____
_____
- Does God know our thoughts? *1 Chronicles 28:9*
- How can we align our thought with Gods Word?
- Is God always thinking about us?
- Where in the Bible does it talk about God's thoughts?
- How do I surrender my thoughts to God?

CHEW ON THIS: If God's thoughts for us are filled with peace, shouldn't we also be able to experience that same peace in our minds when we think about Him? He is the Prince of Peace.

On you own: *Write it down!*
Psalm 33:11_____
_____
Jeremiah 29:11_____
_____
Psalm 40:17 _____
_____
Isaiah 49:16 _____
_____

LEARN & LIVE IT
What is the most important thing God wants from us?
God expects us to accept His Son, the Lord Jesus Christ, as our Saviour. He expects us to give our lives to Him, and in so doing, develop the character of Christ. God wants us to become more like Christ.

LESSON 4
GOD IS THINKING ABOUT YOU!

CONCLUSION
God's thoughts toward us are thoughts of peace and not of evil. He doesn't sit in heaven thinking of ways to take us out because of all the things we've done wrong.

CLOSE IN PRAYER!!

WEEKLY QUIET TIME

DAY	BIBLE PASSAGE	SHARE YOUR DISCOVERIES BELOW
Monday	Psalm 11	
Tuesday	Jeremiah 29:11	
Wednesday	Proverbs 1: 1-7	
Thursday	Proverbs 1: 8-19	
Friday	Proverbs 1: 20 -26	
Saturday	Proverbs 1: 27 -33	

LESSON 5
REVIEW 1

TAKE A STEP BACK & REWIND
It is time to review lessons 1– 4.
- Ask your teacher about the topics you don't understand.
- Be ready to participate and answer the questions for discussion.

CLASS DISCUSSION
- What would you say to a friend who wants to know about your Christian faith?
- Can you explain the topic that challenges you the most?
- What did you learn from the previous lessons?
- Name two topics from the previous lessons.
- Please share the most significant change you've experienced based on previous chapters.
- Feel free to ask questions for more clarity on any of the previous lessons.

WEEKLY QUIET TIME

DAY	BIBLE PASSAGE	SHARE YOUR DISCOVERIES BELOW
Monday	Colossians 1:1-9	
Tuesday	Colossians 1: 10 -20	
Wednesday	Colossians 1: 21-29	
Thursday	Isaiah 7: 1 – 8	
Friday	Isaiah 7: 9 – 17	
Saturday	Isaiah 7: 18 -25	

LESSON 6
DO YOU BELIEVE IN MIRACLES?

 MAIN POINT: Miracles were an important element in the ministry of Jesus Christ. They are not only divine acts, but they are also a form of teaching.

BIBLE READING

John 4: 46-54 & John 6:5-14

MEMORY VERSE

"For with God nothing will be impossible." Luke 1:37

INTRODUCTION
Have you ever told yourself or someone you know, "Well this is going to take a miracle!"? Here's the good news, that's exactly what Jesus wants to do for you. Everything that He does is supernatural because He is a supernatural God.

CLASS ACTIVITY
Rule: No put-downs or negative things can be said or done to anyone. The goal of this game is for each person to feel a part of the group. Winning is not as important as supporting and encouraging each other to live out their faith in Jesus Christ.

Divide the class into two groups and have each group act out without saying a word about the miracles. Each group should guess and write on a sheet of paper what miracle of Jesus has been acted upon.

Teachers should choose one of the miracles of Jesus different from the passages below!

CLASS DISCUSSION
Read and examine the passages below together and tell the class about the life LESSON and application as of today.
- Healing of the official's son, John 4: 46-54.
- Feeding the 5,000 in John 6:5-14.

LESSON 6
DO YOU BELIEF IN MIRACLES?

Discuss the following questions:
- Have you experienced miracles?
- Which is the greatest miracle of all?
- Do you believe the miracle accounts in the Bible?
- Have you ever prayed for a miracle? Why or why not?
- Does a lack of miracles indicate that I do not have enough faith?
- Should we be praying for miracles like they did in ACTS 4:30?
- Does God still perform miracles today?

Write down your take home from today's lesson: _____
_____
_____

CONCLUSION
Miracles are possible by God, and we can still experience them today

CLOSE IN PRAYER!!

WEEKLY QUIET TIME

DAY	BIBLE PASSAGE	SHARE YOUR DISCOVERIES BELOW
Monday	Genesis 1:1-13	
Tuesday	Genesis 1: 14-27	
Wednesday	Genesis 5:24	
Thursday	Hebrews 11:1-5	
Friday	Genesis 21:1-7	
Saturday	Joshua 10:1-12	

LESSON 7
WARNING!

MAIN POINT: Better than seeking after a new miracle is taking God at His Word.

BIBLE READING

2 Corinthians 11:13-14

INTRODUCTION
Some people seek after signs and wonders because they seek an occasion to excuse their unbelief, but it is nobler in God's sight to believe without needing a miracle.

MEMORY VERSE

"Then Jesus told him, "Because you have seen me, you have believed; blessed are those who have not seen and yet have believed." John 20:29

CLASS DISCUSSION
- What does the Bible say about demonic/satanic miracles?
- Do miracles prove that God is working?
- In the Bible, miracles followed the apostles and were evidence of the presence of God – Read Acts 2:43; Acts 5:12; Matthew. 10:1
- What Bible verse can support the statement "False teachers can perform false miracles?"
- Do miracles prove God – Matthew 7:22-23
- Write the following Scriptures in your own words:
- Matthew. 24:24 _____
  _____
- 2 Corinthians. 11:13 -14 _____
  _____

KNOW THIS: When Moses and Aaron confronted Pharaoh, they performed a miraculous sign to confirm their message from God (Exodus 7:8–10).
- The magi of Egypt were able to perform the same miracle "by their secret arts" (verse 11).
- God's miracle was shown to be greater (verse 12), but the fact is that the magi were able to perform a satanic miracle in the king's court.

LESSON 7
WARNING!

CHEW ON THIS
1 John 4:1-3; Any time we are in doubt, we are to make sure that what is being taught agrees with what the Scripture says.

CONCLUSION
Miracles can be counterfeited. That is why God points us to His Word. Signs and wonders can lead us astray. God's Word will always light the true path; Psalm 119:105. Simple faith is more pleasing to the Lord; John 20:29.

CLOSE IN PRAYER!!

Teacher's Corner: *Keep a list of your beloved Teenagers on your desk. Every day, pick one kid and pray for him or her.*

📖 WEEKLY QUIET TIME

DAY	BIBLE PASSAGE	SHARE YOUR DISCOVERIES BELOW
Monday	Genesis 7:1-12	
Tuesday	Genesis 7: 13-24	
Wednesday	Genesis 8:1- 12	
Thursday	Genesis 8: 13- 22	
Friday	Genesis 11: 1-9	
Saturday	Hebrews 11:5	

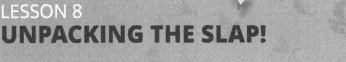

LESSON 8
UNPACKING THE SLAP!

 MAIN POINT: Lack of self-control is a recipe for disaster.

INTRODUCTION
We need Christ and the work of the Holy Spirit to develop consistent self-control in each of us.

CLASS ACTIVITY
If you could have any job in the world; what would you choose? Why?

Attention: Please allow students to watch on their phones!
https://youtu.be/myjEoDypUD8 *Uncensored actor Will Smith slap comedian Chris Rock.*

CLASS DISCUSSION
- What do you think Proverbs 25:28 means? Also, 2 Peter 1:5-7, 1 Timothy 4:12.
- How many of us wouldn't like to have a little more self-control or self-discipline in our lives?
- What is self-control and why is it important?
- Why did you think Will Smith acted the way he did?
- How would you react if the Will Smith-like emotion wells up within you?
- How was Chris Rock able to hold it together?
- Decisions have consequences. What was the consequence for Will Smith?
- Who in the Bible showed self-control?
- How do you develop self-control?
- Who lacked self-control in the Bible?
- How does self-control help you avoid and overcome temptation?

 BIBLE READING

Proverbs 16:32 & Galatians 5:22-23

 MEMORY VERSE

"A fool is quick-tempered, but a wise person stays calm when insulted." Proverbs 12:16

LESSON 8
UNPACKING THE SLAP!

- Do we need God's help to demonstrate self-control?
- Can we do it on our own? Why or why not? *Think about an area of your life where you need God's help.*
- How does learning self-control in your teenage years help you as an adult?

REALITY CHECK

Students get physically out of control and sometimes enter fights in school, home, church, bus ride, and just about everywhere. There are college students with $30K in credit card debt and teenagers who go riotous spending at malls and online. Do any of these describe you?

CONCLUSION

Self-Control is essential in all aspects of life; remember, self-control is a fruit of the Spirit and that means it is a product or result of the work of God's Spirit in your life. We play a part by cooperating with the Holy Spirit in His renewing work in our lives.

ACTION: Pray for the Holy Spirit to assist you in exercising self-control. If there are aspects of your life where self-control has been lacking, repent and don't be discouraged by past failures. God is always calling you to draw closer to Him.

CLOSE IN PRAYER!!

WEEKLY QUIET TIME

DAY	BIBLE PASSAGE	SHARE YOUR DISCOVERIES BELOW
Monday	1 Corinthians 9:24-27	
Tuesday	Galatians 5:22	
Wednesday	Proverbs 16:22	
Thursday	2 Peter 1:6	
Friday	Proverbs 25:28	
Saturday	Romans 12:1-2	

LESSON 9
UKRAINE

MAIN POINT: There is one thing we can do to end this violence; let's be committed to praying for Ukraine!

INTRODUCTION
As Martin Luther King, Jr said: "Injustice anywhere is a threat to justice everywhere. No one is free until all are free!" The Bible instructs us to care for our brothers and sisters, but also pray for those who hate us, remembering that we must do both during the assault on Ukraine by Russia.

CLASS DISCUSSION
- Are you ready to shift your focus from yourself to others? What would this mean in practice?
- What exactly does the Bible say about the future? Are we in the end times?
- How can we be of help in times of war?
- Can you commit to prayer?
- What can we learn from what Jesus said in Matthew 24:4-8?
- "Do not worry about tomorrow for tomorrow will worry about itself each day has enough trouble of its own" Matthew 6:34? How can we make this our reality?
- Luke 6:35-36 (MSG)"I tell you, love your enemies. Help and give without expecting a return. You'll never – I promise – regret it. Live out this God-created identity the way our Father lives toward us, generously and graciously, even when we're at our worst. Our Father is kind; you be kind." What is this passage saying to you?

BIBLE READING

Ecclesiastes 3:1-8

MEMORY VERSE

"For everything there is a season, a time for every activity under heaven."
Ecclesiastes 3:1

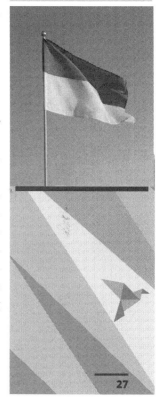

LESSON 9
UKRAINE

KNOW THIS: Some end-time signs are near:
- Humanity is in danger of self-destruction
- Tensions over Jerusalem and the Temple Mount are growing!
- The gospel of the Kingdom of God is being preached (Matthew 24:14)
- Things that have not happened yet (but could happen suddenly)
- Jesus said in Matthew 24:34, "This generation [apparently the generation that 'sees all these things,' verse 33] will by no means pass away till all these things take place." This sets an outer limit of a generation for these end-time events. But He also said, "But of that day and hour no one knows, not even the angels of heaven, but My Father only" (verse 36).

A CALL TO ACTION: Read Matthew chapters 24 and 25, Jesus addressed much more about what we should be doing.

ACTION: I commit to praying for the Russia-Ukraine Conflict in the following ways _____

You can also help by giving online at "**GiveNowToSave.org**"

CONCLUSION

What should we be doing? Study about the faithful servant (Matthew 24:45-51), the five wise virgins (Matthew 25:1-13), the good and profitable servants (verses 14-30), and the generous and serving "sheep" (verses 31-46). Strive to be like them and not like their evil, foolish, unprofitable, and uncompassionate counterparts.

CLOSE IN PRAYER!

Teacher's Corner: Reminder: when a teen asks you to pray for him or her, please stop right then and pray for that specific teenager.

WEEKLY QUIET TIME

DAY	BIBLE PASSAGE	SHARE YOUR DISCOVERIES BELOW
Monday	Leviticus 6:13	
Tuesday	2 Samuel 12:10	
Wednesday	Psalm 31:1	
Thursday	Psalm 55:22	
Friday	Psalm 71:1	
Saturday	Psalm 23	

LESSON 10
SOCIETY, SELF & FAMILY

 MAIN POINT: Can we always turn to the Scripture for practical living in all areas?

BIBLE READING

Proverbs 4:1-9

INTRODUCTION
It is important to follow God's Plan for our lives! If we're not careful with the people who influence us, we could end up farther away from God than we could ever imagine. Our lives will not be good if our closest companions are people who do not fear God, who are not walking with God, or not seeking to glorify God.

MEMORY VERSE

"For we live by believing and not by seeing" 2 Corinthians 5:7 (NLT)

Write down one of your "MEMORY Versed" Scriptures.

_____

_____

CLASS DISCUSSION
SOCIETY (Read Proverbs 29:18)
- How can we turn to the Scripture for a practical living?
- What is a Christian's role in society (COMMUNITY)?
- What does the Bible say about family in society?
- What three major problems do you think society is facing today?
- How should Christians handle these problems?
- Does our faith make a difference?

Chew on this: Society has its own culture and ways of life that totally deviate from Christian views.

SELF (Read Matthew 16:24)
- What is your role in the society?

LESSON 10
SOCIETY, SELF & FAMILY

- Can LOVE make our community a better place?
- What does the Bible say about family love and family unity?
- Genesis 2:20-25, Genesis 4:1, Hebrews 12:14
- What practical steps can we take to love one another?

_____
_____

FAMILY (Read Joshua 24:14-15)
- What do you think is the biggest problem with redefining the family structure?
- What is our role in making sure the love of Christ is evident in our own lives?
- Why are we more likely to be critical of the Scripture than the media?
- What kind of wrong conclusions do we experience when we follow the lies that others believe?

CHEW ON THIS: We all can make a difference and make the world a better place!

ACTION: Here are three practical ways you can put your faith into action today:
- Release your faith through what you pray. Prayer is the greatest privilege we have! Luke 18:1
- Release your faith through what you say, Matthew 5:37
- Release your faith through what you do; Colossians 3:23-24

LEARN IT AND LIVE IT: Following God's Plan for Your Life:
- Read the Word actively!
- Follow the commands He puts on your heart!
- Seek a godly community!
- Obey the Truth of God's Word!

CONCLUSION
Family is at the center of God's plan for the happiness and progress of His children. The Holy Bible teaches that God established families from the very beginning, and it shows us many examples of strong families.

LESSON 10
SOCIETY, SELF & FAMILY

CLOSE IN PRAYER!!

📖 WEEKLY QUIET TIME

DAY	BIBLE PASSAGE	SHARE YOUR DISCOVERIES BELOW
Monday	James 2:20	
Tuesday	Philippians 3:8	
Wednesday	Romans 12:2	
Thursday	1 John 2:15	
Friday	John 2:15	
Saturday	1 Corinthians 13:4-7	

THE BIBLE AND SOCIETY!

As Christians, how can we make sense of our world, our relationships, and our faith without some knowledge and understanding of the Bible? Well, I guess we can't!

This Book is the Word of God. In it, He makes known to men His character and will. It is all given by inspiration of the Holy Ghost and is profitable; teaching men what to believe; showing them in what they are wrong; instructing them in what is right; and leading them, through the grace of God, to do it. (2 Tim. 3:16 -17)

Although written by men, God directed them to write and how to write it. It is perfect! Having been all written, not in words taught by the wisdom of men, but the wisdom of God, it is "perfect, converting the soul; sure, making wise the simple; and right, rejoicing the heart." – Psalms 19:7-14

Of course, the knowledge of this book is more to be desired than gold, even much fine gold; because in understanding, believing, and obeying it, there is a great present and a great future reward.

Let's dive into God's word!

Much love to you!
Pastor Moji Olagbegi

LESSON 11
FREEZE

MAIN POINT: What are the benefits of following God's instructions?

BIBLE READING
Matthew 4:18-20

INTRODUCTION
Jesus said "Are you tired? Worn out? Burned out on religion? Come to me. Get away with me and you'll recover your life. I'll show you how to take a real rest. Walk with me and work with me — watch how I do it. Learn the unforced rhythms of grace. I won't lay anything heavy or ill-fitting on you. Keep company with me and you'll learn to live freely and lightly."

MEMORY VERSE

"Long ago the LORD said to Israel: "I have loved you, my people, with an everlasting love. With unfailing love, I have drawn you to myself" Jeremiah 31:3.

CLASS ACTIVITY (FREEZE FRAME)
TEACHERS: Based on the party game of musical statues. Invite the youths to quietly move around the room and await your instructions. As they are walking the leader calls out popular Bible names like King David, Joseph, Judas, Martha, Moses, Joshua, Deborah, Mary Magdalene, and Goliath; and when they hear the name, they must stop immediately and hold a still 'freeze frame' illustrating or acting out the name.

CLASS DISCUSSION
Read Deuteronomy 12:28; Ephesians 6:1-3; Matthew 28:19-20; Luke 11:28; Colossians 3:20
- What did you learn from the freeze game?
- Give an example of how something might go wrong if you don't follow instructions.
- Write at least four reasons why obedience to God is important!
- Write two reasons why following instructions in sports is not negotiable!

LESSON 11
FREEZE

CONCLUSION

If you were given instructions on how to sing a song, it might be okay to do it your own way instead. But if God gives you instructions, you had better follow those instructions! There are many times when we might feel like doing things our own way would be best, but choosing to not follow instructions often ends in a disaster. God sees a much bigger picture than we do (He knows everything!), so we can trust that God's way is really the best way.

CLOSE IN PRAYER!!
Psalm 119:105, Ecclesiastes 12

WEEKLY QUIET TIME

DAY	BIBLE PASSAGE	SHARE YOUR DISCOVERIES BELOW
Monday	Proverbs 4:20-27	
Tuesday	Hebrews 2:1-3	
Wednesday	Hebrews 11:1-10	
Thursday	Hebrews 11:11-20	
Friday	Hebrews 11:21-30	
Saturday	Hebrews 11:31-40	

LESSON 12
FIRST INTERACTIVE SESSION AND QUIZ 1

Dear Teachers,

Please note the following:
- Make the interactive session interesting.
- Ensure the teens participate by allowing them to contribute and state what they have learned as well as ask questions.
- Prepare your own questions and quiz that you will ask them based on the previous lessons.
- You may give gifts to those who perform well in the quiz.
- Create an avenue for the teens to give useful suggestions on how the Sunday School Class can be improved.

Below are some suggested questions you can ask— feel free to add to them!
- Mention five or more previous lesson topics.
- Ask if they remember the Bible passages of each lesson.
- Ask them to recite the memory verses.
- Ask questions from the Activities session as well.
- Ask them questions on the body of the lessons.

WEEKLY QUIET TIME

DAY	BIBLE PASSAGE	SHARE YOUR DISCOVERIES BELOW
Monday	Psalm 119:97-100	
Tuesday	Psalm 119:101-104	
Wednesday	Psalm 119:105	
Thursday	Ecclesiastes 12:1-3	
Friday	Ecclesiastes 12:4-7	
Saturday	Ecclesiastes 12:8-14	

THE ZEAL FOR TEENS | 2023/2024

LESSON 13
HONEST TALK

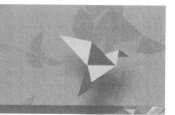

BIBLE READING

Proverbs 26:12

MEMORY VERSE

"Casting all your anxieties on him, because he cares for you." 1 Peter 5:7

MAIN POINT: We all need to help each other.

INTRODUCTION
To begin with, the identities we develop on social media do not represent our true selves. Most of the pictures posted on these sites are cropped and filtered to portray to nonexistent realities. Social media has its place but cannot and must not replace the real-life community support and help we can lean on in times of trouble.

CLASS DISCUSSION
Today's class discussion is to help us pour out our minds and get help!

Instruction:
1. Divide the class into two separate groups: Male vs. Female.
2. Teachers should have students write their questions on a paper without giving out their names.
3. We must be honest and respectful of each other.
4. Pray that God will take away the insecurity and lies in the class.

In each group discuss the following:
- Read Ecclesiastes 11:9-10
  - Why do teenagers refuse to ask for help?
  - What happens when we keep it all in?
  - Do we present our real selves on social media?

- Read 2 Corinthians 10:12
  - What is a manipulated self?

LESSON 13
HONEST TALK

- How do social media give us a false sense of reality?
- Are people different from social media than in real life?
- Describe how media affects people's perception of reality?
- Please pray together right now
- Pray for your teachers too!

Some negative effects of social media (you can add to the list)
- Distraction
- Loneliness
- Disrupted sleep
- Exposure to bullying
- Rumor spreading
- Unrealistic views of other people's lives and peer pressure.
- Negative self-perception and mental health

The more we consume on social media the more sensitive we become to the content we watch. We start believing that the pictures and videos we watch are real – when subconsciously we all know they are edited, or only represent one small part of reality.

ACTION: Speak out and have an accountability adult; you have to trust the eyes, wisdom, and the godly experience around you. Our community is here to support you. We care for you!

CONCLUSION
Remember that you're loved! You need godly mentors. God doesn't expect you to do this all on your own. He wants you to have a mentor to help you in your life.

Note to teachers: For next week's lesson, you will need to invite two to three young adults (20-39 years old) from your church to share their life experiences with the youths; please plan!

LESSON 13
HONEST TALK

📖 WEEKLY QUIET TIME

DAY	BIBLE PASSAGE	SHARE YOUR DISCOVERIES BELOW
Monday	Acts 8:30-35	
Tuesday	John 10:11	
Wednesday	John 3:16-17	
Thursday	Romans 5:8	
Friday	Matthew 12:9-14	
Saturday	Matthew 12:15-21	

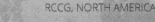

LESSON 14
SENIOR SUNDAY

MAIN POINT: Decisions made in High School will affect your life personally!

ADVICE WITH LOVE: The decisions you make in college matter. People often think of college as a time of freedom — a time to do whatever they want without facing consequences. However, what you do in college matters. Once you graduate, the day after graduation, when you're in the real world, it's not like you start clean – with a clean record. Instead, you are a summation of all the decisions you've made over your four years in college. I know it's scary, but if you are a senior in high school or just starting in college, make sure you view college in the right way.

BIBLE READING

Galatians 4:16

MEMORY VERSE

"Jesus Christ is the same yesterday and today and forever." Hebrews 13:8

CLASS DISCUSSION
Note to teacher: Let the two to three Young Adults (20-39 years) you invited share their life experiences with the youth!

TALK IT OVER
- Taking Jesus to High School and College starts right now!
- Choose the right college and degree for you!
- Hard work and good discipline equal good grades!
- Pray for God's favor and college scholarship!
- Learn time management and good discipline!
- In college, set boundaries together with your roommates!
- Be intentional about the friends you make (godly values)
- Stay in the Word — Romans 1:16, Joshua 1:9.

LESSON 14
SENIOR SUNDAY

- Make decisions for your destiny, not for temporary desires!
- You don't need the credit cards offered in college!
- Find yourself a church (your parents are not here to drag you)
- Find a good Bible study group (community) Proverbs 9:10
- Decisions do have good rewards or bad consequences.
- Set personal boundaries — DON'T MAKE DECISION BASED ON FEELINGS.
- Pray about everything — pray daily for protection.

ACTION: Get a calendar and learn how to effectively manage a to-do list. Build a little discipline...it will go a long way. Psalm 25:4-5

CONCLUSION
The quickest path away from God is to pursue yourself and your own interests.

CLOSE IN PRAYER!!
WEEKLY QUIET TIME

DAY	BIBLE PASSAGE	SHARE YOUR DISCOVERIES BELOW
Monday	Philippians 3:12-14	
Tuesday	John 8:36	
Wednesday	1 Corinthians 6:12	
Thursday	Psalm 32:8	
Friday	Acts 13:38-39	
Saturday	Romans 6:22	

LESSON 15
GOD, I WISH SOMEBODY WOULD'VE TOLD ME THIS WHEN I WAS YOUNGER!

 MAIN POINT: Don't go after a dream that is not in God's plan for you.

BIBLE READING

Jeremiah 29:11

INTRODUCTION
There are two phrases many people often say in their lives, "I wish I could… and, I wish I had…," What they are really saying is, "I'm unhappy with the choices that I've made."

MEMORY VERSE

"Many are the plans in the mind of a man, but it is the purpose of the LORD that will stand." Proverbs 19:21 (ESV)

CLASS ACTIVITY
- Name a gift you will never forget? Please make sure everyone participates!

Know this song? "Victoria's Secret" is a song by American singer and songwriter Jax – and produced by Jesse Siebenberg and Mark Nilan. It was released in June 2022 – to all streaming platforms – after being previously teased on TikTok and performed at Governors Ball Music Festival earlier that month. The song has charted internationally and the first line of the song is; "God, I wish somebody would've told me."

**** Please this is a dirty secular song so pardon the language but use it for life LESSON! ****

VICTORIA SECRET LYRICS by Jax
God, I wish somebody would've told me
When I was younger that all bodies aren't the same
Photoshop itty bitty models on magazine covers
Told me I was overweight
I stopped eating, what a bummer
Can't have carbs in a hot girl summer

LESSON 15
GOD, I WISH SOMEBODY WOULD'VE TOLD ME THIS WHEN I WAS YOUNGER!

If I could go back and tell myself
When I was younger, I'd say, "Psst
I know Victoria's secret
And, girl, you wouldn't believe
She's an old man who lives in Ohio
Making money off of girls like me"
Cashin' in on body issues
Sellin' skin and bones with big boobs
I know Victoria's secret
She was made up by a dude (dude)
Victoria was made up by a dude (dude)
Victoria was made up by a dude
I wish somebody would've told me that thighs of thunder
Meant normal human thighs
The fuckin' pressure I was under
To lose my appetite
And fight the cellulite with Hunger Games like every night
If I could go back and tell myself
When I was younger, I'd say
"Hey, dummy"

CLASS DISCUSSION
- What is the message of the lyrics?
- Think about anything in your life that detracts you from following truthful advice wholeheartedly.
- How are we nurturing our own intimacy with the truth we're being told?
- Ponder on Philippians 4:8.
- Think about a small thing that you can do to make better decisions!

REALITY CHECK: What did you learn from today's class? Remember God has a standard that can never change.

CHALLENGE:
- The Holy Spirit has a duty and responsibility to God to lead and guide you into all truths.
- Ask God for grace to apply truthful information even when it hurts!

LESSON 15
GOD, I WISH SOMEBODY WOULD'VE TOLD ME THIS WHEN I WAS YOUNGER!

- Serve the Lord God with all your heart!

ACTION: Write yourself a letter that will help you never to repeat the same mess or mistakes from other people's lives. LEARN FROM HISTORY!

CONCLUSION
Your Decisions today may mark the future that you have tomorrow. The truth is hard to take – sometimes, it hurts people and makes them uneasy but is needed!

WEEKLY QUIET TIME

DAY	BIBLE PASSAGE	SHARE YOUR DISCOVERIES BELOW
Monday	Psalm 119:9-16	
Tuesday	Luke 6:37	
Wednesday	Matthew 18:21-22	
Thursday	Psalm 86:5	
Friday	Mark 11:25	
Saturday	Psalm 119: 17-24	

THE ZEAL FOR TEENS | 2023/2024

LESSON 16
HOW TO BE BLESSED

BIBLE READING
Matthew 5: 3-10

MEMORY VERSE
"And so, dear brothers and sisters, I plead with you to give your bodies to God because of all he has done for you. Let them be a living and holy sacrifice – the kind he will find acceptable. This is truly the way to worship him." Romans 12:1

MAIN POINT: Many of us hear or use the phrase "be blessed" but do we really know what it means?

INTRODUCTION
Jesus uses the term "blessed" in His most famous sermon, the Sermon on the Mount, in a section often called the "Beatitudes." In the Beatitudes, Jesus totally shocks us with a much different version of a blessing than many expect. He shows us how being blessed is much different than everything going well for us. In fact, we can be blessed even when everything seems to be going wrong.

CLASS ACTIVITY
Ice Breaker: Are there ways that you feel you don't fit in with the stereotypes about your generation? What are some things that people seem to assume about your Gen Z? How many of these do you think are accurate?

CLASS DISCUSSION
EXPLORING THE BEATITUDES: When Jesus saw His ministry drawing huge crowds, He climbed a hillside. Those who were apprenticed to Him, the committed, climbed with Him. Arriving at a quiet place, He sat down and taught His climbing companions. This is what He said:
Mathew 5:3-10 (MSG)
- 3. "You're blessed when you're at the end of your rope. With less of you there is more of God and his rule.

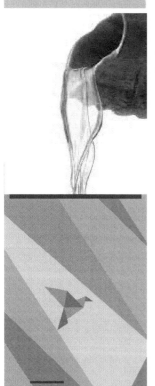

LESSON 16
HOW TO BE BLESSED

- 4. "You're blessed when you feel you've lost what is most dear to you. Only then can you be embraced by the One most dear to you.
- 5 "You're blessed when you're content with just who you are—no more, no less. That's the moment you find yourselves proud owners of everything that can't be bought.
- 6 "You're blessed when you've worked up a good appetite for God. He's food and drink in the best meal you'll ever eat.
- 7 "You're blessed when you care. At the moment of being 'care-full,' you find yourselves cared for.
- 8 "You're blessed when you get your inside world—your mind and heart—put right. Then you can see God in the outside world.
- 9 "You're blessed when you can show people how to cooperate instead of compete or fight. That's when you discover who you really are, and your place in God's family.
- 10 "You're blessed when your commitment to God provokes persecution. The persecution drives you even deeper into God's kingdom.

Discuss the following questions:
- What is the main message of the Beatitude?
- Does this teaching challenge your view of what it means to be blessed?
- How will you apply the Beatitude in your everyday life?
- Is the teaching still applicable to us today? If Yes or No Explain.
- What are the four most important teachings in the Beatitudes?
- What did Jesus teach you in the Beatitudes? Write below.

_____
_____
_____

ACTION: At home, write each verse of Beatitudes in your words Matthew 5:3-10!

CHEW ON THIS: The Beatitudes help us better understand the blessing God has in store for us and what it means to be a follower of Jesus.

LESSON 16
HOW TO BE BLESSED

CONCLUSION
Jesus uses the Beatitudes to speak to a variety of listeners and to communicate several messages about the Kingdom of Heaven. The emphasis is on righteousness that begins with the transformation of the inner life and then moves to conform external behavior to inward values.

CLOSE IN PRAYER!!

WEEKLY QUIET TIME

DAY	BIBLE PASSAGE	SHARE YOUR DISCOVERIES BELOW
Monday	Philippians 4:13	
Tuesday	Isaiah 12:2	
Wednesday	Ephesians 3:20	
Thursday	Psalm 119:1-8	
Friday	Philemon 1:4-8	
Saturday	Philippians 4:8	

LESSON 17
KNOW YOUR TEACHERS!

 MAIN POINT: Appreciate your teachers!

INTRODUCTION
We teach and lead because God has called us to do so. For thousands of years, God has asked and equipped teachers to participate in the work of helping others come to know God and live as people of faith.

CLASS ACTIVITY
Icebreaker: A woman gives an astronaut $1, the woman is the astronaut's sister, but the astronaut is not the woman's brother, why?

Note to teachers: This class will comprise 2 sections: (1) Questions for Teachers; and (2) Questions for Students

QUESTIONS FOR TEACHER(S)
Have the student write their questions for the teacher(s) on a sticky note and place it in a basket. Allow 20 minutes for students to ask questions.

QUESTION FOR STUDENTS
- What is your favorite thing in the Youth group?
- Explain 1 Corinthians 12:28 & 2 Timothy 3:16
- How can we improve our teacher-student relationship?
- A year from now, how would you like to be more Christ-like?
- What small thing could you do for the Youth group this week?
- Consider one way you can encourage godly fellowship?
- Who is a model of Christlikeness in your life?

BIBLE READING
Proverbs 9:9

MEMORY VERSE
"The student is not above the teacher, but everyone who is fully trained will be like their teacher" Luke 6:40

LESSON 17
KNOW YOUR TEACHERS!

- What do you appreciate about your teacher?

ACTION: Write a kind note today with Bible verses for teachers to brighten their day and show them the fruit of their hard work and dedication to their students!

Advice for Teachers: "Good preaching requires teaching. And good teaching requires patience. Good teachers don't issue the final exam on the first day of class. They begin where the students are and don't reject them, or demean them, or write them off for their ignorance of a subject they are yet to learn. Rather, they seek to inform them, and change them – to improve and move and advance them – through the work of teaching". — **John Piper**

CONCLUSION
Teachers are some of the most selfless, giving, caring individuals in our world. Their goals and ambitions are in seeing their students succeed in life. And many of us have our teachers to thank for where we are! Yet, teachers often face discouragement and feelings of defeat. Speak words of encouragement and thankfulness to the teachers you know, and it will make a difference in their day.

CLOSE IN PRAYER!!

WEEKLY QUIET TIME

DAY	BIBLE PASSAGE	SHARE YOUR DISCOVERIES BELOW
Monday	1 John 2:27	
Tuesday	Psalms 132:12	
Wednesday	Psalm 119:99	
Thursday	Psalm 32:1-8	
Friday	Psalm 27: 1-6	
Saturday	Psalm 27: 7-14	

LESSON 18
REVIEW 2

TAKE A STEP BACK & REWIND

It is time to review lessons 13 - 17.
- Ask your teacher about the topics you don't understand.
- Be ready to participate and answer the questions for discussion.

CLASS DISCUSSION
- What would you say to a friend who wants to know about your Christian faith?
- Can you explain the topic that challenges you the most?
- What did you learn from the previous lesson?
- Name two topics from the previous lessons.
- Please share the most significant change you've experienced based on previous chapters.
- Feel free to ask questions for more clarity on any of the previous lessons.

WEEKLY QUIET TIME

DAY	BIBLE PASSAGE	SHARE YOUR DISCOVERIES BELOW
Monday	Ruth 1:1-5	
Tuesday	Ruth 1:6 - 9	
Wednesday	Ruth 1:10-13	
Thursday	Ruth 1:14-18	
Friday	Ruth 1: 19-22	
Saturday	Joshua 1:5	

THE ZEAL FOR TEENS | 2023/2024

LESSON 19
ENGAGING WITH SCRIPTURE

BIBLE READING
Psalm 119:9-16

MEMORY VERSE
"Joyful are people of integrity, who follow the instructions of the Lord" Psalm 119:1

MAIN POINT: Consider the condition of your heart.

INTRODUCTION
Lord, please help me to trust You more and give me the strength to live life as You intended and to fulfill Your purpose for me on earth. Help me to live in Your light and feel the blessings You freely bestow on me.

CLASS ACTIVITY
Ice Breaker: What do you wish older people understood better about you specifically, and younger people in general?

CLASS DISCUSSION
⁹"How can a young person stay pure? By obeying your word.
¹⁰ I have tried hard to find you— don't let me wander from your commands.
¹¹ I have hidden your word in my heart, that I might not sin against you.
¹² I praise you, O LORD; teach me your decrees.
¹³ I have recited aloud all the regulations you have given us.
¹⁴ I have rejoiced in your laws as much as in riches.
¹⁵ I will study your commandments and reflect on your ways.
¹⁶ I will delight in your decrees and not forget your word." Psalm 119:9-16 (NLT)

Now read Psalm 119: 1- 16 and discuss the following questions:
- Who is verse nine speaking to?

LESSON 19
ENGAGING WITH SCRIPTURE

- What does it mean to keep one's way pure?
- How do we keep our way according to God's Word?
- What does Psalm119: verse 1 and verse 9 have in common?
- What does it mean to pursue the Lord and how?
- What happens if we are also seeking something else?
- Can we seek God with our whole heart on our own?
- What happens when we don't follow God's direction?
- How is verse 2 parallel to verse 10?
- Why should we treasure God's Word in our heart? And how can we do that?
- How does God's Word keep us from sinning?
- How is verse 3 parallel to verse 11?

ACTION:
- Seek God with all your heart!
- Keep God's Word in your heart!
- Meditate on God's Word

REFLECT: Personally, do you believe you are currently living in a gray or lukewarm world? Why or why not?

CONCLUSION
God loves you and has great plans for you. Work to discover your purpose on earth as God intended and live in the light of fulfilling the special plans God has for you.

CLOSE IN PRAYER!!

WEEKLY QUIET TIME

DAY	BIBLE PASSAGE	SHARE YOUR DISCOVERIES BELOW
Monday	Prov. 1:1– 9	
Tuesday	1 Timothy 4:7– 16	
Wednesday	Psalm 119: 1-8	
Thursday	Psalm 119: 9-16	
Friday	Psalm 150	
Saturday	1 Samuel 1	

ADVICE TO YOUNG PEOPLE

To the young, I would like to pass on these words of advice.

- Realize you are an awakening personality and take as much interest in the development of your soul as your physical development.
- Character is the most important thing in life, and Jesus is the master architect of Character.
- Cleverness and education may get you to the top but only character will keep you there.
- Find a cause to which you can dedicate yourself wholeheartedly.
- Set clear goals for yourself – don't drift. Some people allow circumstances or friends to dictate what they do in life.
- Don't react – act.
- Prayer is an essential part of life.
- PRAY: Dear God my Father, may I pass through each stage of my life knowing Your guiding and protective hand is upon me.

— *Advice from* **Selwyn Hughes.**

LESSON 20 (ACTIVITY)
DOUBTING THOMAS

 MAIN POINT: We are not alone when we long for evidence for our faith.

INTRODUCTION
We all doubt from time to time. Doubt itself is not sinful or wrong. It often can be the catalyst to new spiritual growth. The gospel shows us that even in the midst of our worst doubt, Jesus is able to draw closer to us than we could possibly imagine. Jesus does this very thing with His doubting disciple Thomas in John 20.

CLASS ACTIVITY
- Divide the class into two or more teams.
- Each person at a time from a team is given a chance to tell the opposing team something about himself/herself.
- Each person may choose to say something that is true or something that is false. For example, someone could say, "My favorite food is my mom's fried rice"!
- The other team will try to guess if the person is telling the truth. If they think he/she is lying, they'll say, "We doubt it." If they think he/she is telling the truth, they'll say, "We believe you."
- If the person sharing the info fools the opposing team, his/her team gets a point. If the other team guesses correctly, it gets a point.
- Alternate teams until each person has had a chance to say something about themselves.
- Tally the score and declare a winner.

BIBLE READING

John 20:24-29

MEMORY VERSE

"He sent forth His word and healed them; He rescued them from the Pit." Psalm 107:20

LESSON 20 (ACTIVITY)
DOUBTING THOMAS

CLASS DISCUSSION
- How is this game like trying to decide whether to believe what Jesus says? How is it different?
- What are some things that you have doubted in the Bible? About God?
- What are some of your doubts?
- Are doubts good or bad?
- Why is Thomas not ashamed to share his doubt with the disciples?
- How did Jesus find out about his doubt?

LEARN IT AND LIVE IT
- Use your doubt to strengthen and grow your faith!
- Admit your doubts and ask for help; *Mark 9:24*
- Recognize that faith is a choice, not a feeling.
- Act on Your Faith, Not Your Doubts.
- Doubt Your Doubts, Not Your Faith.
- There are Some Things You Will Never Understand About This Side of Heaven.

REALITY CHECK
- **Intellectual doubts:** These are doubts most often raised by those outside the Christian faith. Is the Bible the Word of God? Is Jesus the Son of God? Did He really rise from the dead? **Have faith in Christ Jesus and accept His salvation!**
- **Spiritual doubts:** These tend to be the doubts of those inside the church. Am I really a Christian? Have I truly believed? Why is it so hard to pray? Why do I still feel guilty? **The Word of God is True; believe it and act on it!**
- **Circumstantial doubts:** This is the largest category because it encompasses all the "whys" of life. Why did my friend die? Why did my parents break up? Why did my friend betray me? Where was God when I was being abused? These questions touch the intersection of biblical faith and the pain of a fallen world. Always remember, **God is fully in control and loves you!**

LESSON 20 (ACTIVITY)
DOUBTING THOMAS

CONCLUSION
Doubt is not sinful, but it can be dangerous. It can hinder and destroy spiritual growth. It's what you do with your doubt that matters.

WEEKLY QUIET TIME

DAY	BIBLE PASSAGE	SHARE YOUR DISCOVERIES BELOW
Monday	Psalm 107:20	
Tuesday	Matthew 8:9-12	
Wednesday	Genesis 32:10	
Thursday	Matthew 15:26-27	
Friday	Genesis 3:1-11	
Saturday	Genesis 3:12-24	

THE ZEAL FOR TEENS | 2023/2024

LESSON 21
DON'T GIVE IN TO DISTRACTIONS!

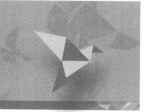

BIBLE READING
Jude 1: 3-10

MEMORY VERSE
"Then he said to the crowd, "If any of you wants to be my follower, you must give up your own way, take up your cross daily, and follow me." Luke 9:23

MAIN POINT: What steps are you willing to take to lessen the distraction?

INTRODUCTION
Distraction is at an all-time high. Busy, busy, busy we are, and this is how the fallen one is attacking us. If he could get us too distracted to follow Christ with all our might, then he is winning the battle in our lives.

CLASS DISCUSSION
This discussion will help show that even though the challenges we face are different from back then, we still have pressing challenges to face, and we need to be willing to overcome them by any means necessary.

- Back in the years after Jesus resurrected, what were the challenges of the church and their followers?
- What were some of the specific challenges they faced?
- What were some of the ways they dealt with these challenges?
- Do we face the same challenges they had?
- What are the challenges we specifically face in living a life centered around Jesus?
- Can our challenges today be compared to back then?
- How are our challenges the same or different?
- Why is it so hard to follow Jesus in our society?
- What are some ways we can stop the distraction in our lives so we can focus on Jesus?

LESSON 21
DON'T GIVE IN TO DISTRACTIONS!

- How can we counter the culture we are living in so that God becomes more prevalent in our lives?

ACTION: Consider ways we can overcome being distracted and spend more time in fellowship with our God.

CONCLUSION
Our challenges are different today than they were back then. But they are still challenges. Jesus promised us He would be with us through our challenges, until the very end of the age. Learning to lean on Him for strength is a lifetime challenge, but oh so worth it in the end.

CLOSE IN PRAYER!!

WEEKLY QUIET TIME

DAY	BIBLE PASSAGE	SHARE YOUR DISCOVERIES BELOW
Monday	Psalm 27:1-6	
Tuesday	Psalm 27: 7-14	
Wednesday	Psalm 36:1-10	
Thursday	Exodus 15:13	
Friday	Joel 2:1-2	
Saturday	Luke 8:1-8	

THE ZEAL FOR TEENS | 2023/2024

LESSON 22
DO YOU SEE YOURSELF AS GOD SEES YOU?

BIBLE READING

Hebrews 12:4-13

MEMORY VERSE

"The Lord is my light and my salvation so why should I be afraid?"
Psalm 27:1

 MAIN POINT: The truth about you is the way God sees you!

INTRODUCTION
When God looks at you, He always sees the unique, fearfully, and wonderful made YOU. Until you see yourself through God's eyes, your view of yourself is NOT the Truth. Don't let anyone, any situation or anything – including your mirror – tell you anything different.

CLASS ACTIVITY
What acrostics can you create using the letters in your name?

An acrostic is an arrangement of words in which certain letters in each line, when taken in order, spell out a word or motto. Or a poem, word puzzle, or other composition in which certain letters in each line form a word or words.

CHECK OUT THE EXAMPLES BELOW
Few examples of acrostics:
DIANE = Dynamic, Independent, Able, No-nonsense and Enthusiastic.
TOLU = Testimony of love unleashed.
GRACE = God's Riches at Christ's Expense
SEYI = Shaping excellence and youthful inside

LET'S THINK THROUGH IT: Why is a name important? Acts 4:10-12, Isaiah 25:1.

Our names are an incredibly important part of our identity. They carry deep personal, cultural, familial, and historical connections. They also give us a

LESSON 22
DO YOU SEE YOURSELF AS GOD SEES YOU?

sense of who we are – the communities in which we belong, and our place in the world.

CLASS DISCUSSION
- Do you love your name? Why or why not?
- Do you think your name is affecting your feeling of self-worth?
- Was there any truth in the words and phrases you chose to represent your name?
- Can you say it is the real me?
- What words and phrases might your friends and family use to describe you?
- What words and phrases would you want people to use to describe you?
- What words might God use to describe you?
- If God promised to add one characteristic or quality to your life, what would you like Him to add? _____
  _____
- Align your view of yourself to God's view; 1 Peter 1:3-4.
- How do you see yourself? Pause for a moment and think about it. What thoughts have you had about yourself today?

CHEW ON THIS: Philippians 2:9
Have you ever wondered; Why the name of Jesus is above every other name? Ultimately, when Paul tells us that Jesus is the Name above all names, it means Jesus' Name is superior, greater, and more powerful than any other name in the world because Jesus is superior, greater, and more powerful than anyone else in the world because He is God (John 1:1).

ACTION: What are some things you can start doing now to start building the type of reputation you want to be remembered by?
Write down your take home from this LESSON!

_____
_____
_____

LESSON 22
DO YOU SEE YOURSELF AS GOD SEES YOU?

CONCLUSION

So many of us find ourselves basing our self-worth on how others see us and, on our accomplishments, feeling shame from our past, defining our value based on our looks, or setting unrealistic standards for ourselves. But it doesn't have to be this way. If only we could see ourselves as God sees us!

CLOSE IN PRAYER!!

WEEKLY QUIET TIME

DAY	BIBLE PASSAGE	SHARE YOUR DISCOVERIES BELOW
Monday	Romans 11: 1-8	
Tuesday	Philippians 2:9	
Wednesday	John 1: 1-14	
Thursday	John 1: 15-18	
Friday	Romans 1: 1-8	
Saturday	1 Corinthians 5:1-7	

LESSON 23
DISTINCTION BETWEEN MORALITY AND CHRISTIANITY

 MAIN POINT: Distinction between doing good deeds out of morals and Christianity.

INTRODUCTION: When we brag about how great we think we are, it places all the attention on our own power and neglects the importance of God's work in our lives. We should in humility focus on Christ first and foremost and remember that our strength comes from Him.

CLASS DISCUSSION
Read Luke 18:9-14, 1 Corinthians 6:19-20
The following definitions will be helpful for today's discussion, please keep them in mind and re-read them as often as needed.

CHRISTIANITY: To be a Christian is to be Christ-filled. This achieves righteousness and helps our growth in the image of Christ.

MORALITY: Morality is a wonderful thing, but it is futile outside of faith in Christ.
- How do you become a Christian?
- Is it okay to do good and reject God's salvation?
- Does good work produce righteousness?
- Can we achieve righteousness our own?
- Why must sound doctrine be the foundation for good deeds? Titus 3:4-7
- Why are the "good deeds" of those in the fraternity and sororities worthless? Titus 3:8
- Why must we insist that to mingle good works with faith for salvation is to pollute the pure gospel of God's grace?

 BIBLE READING

Isaiah 64: 1-7

 MEMORY VERSE

"And you know that God anointed Jesus of Nazareth with the Holy Spirit and with power. Then Jesus went around doing good and healing all who were oppressed by the devil, for God was with him." Acts 10:38

LESSON 23
DISTINCTION BETWEEN MORALITY AND CHRISTIANITY

READ THE STORY (*Curried from Wikipedia*):
The DeCavalcante crime family, also known as the North Jersey Mafia, is an Italian American-Mafia organized crime family that operates mainly in northern New Jersey, particularly in Elizabeth, Newark, West New York, and various other North Jersey cities and the surrounding areas in North Jersey. The family did lots of good deed in his neighborhood. He will without fail give out Thanksgiving turkey and meal for all that comes to the trucks center owned by his family. He is known for paying rents, college tuitions and several key help for his community. But the family that went all out on good deeds has its illicit activities include Bookmaking, cement and construction violations, bootlegging, corruption, drug trafficking, extortion, fencing, fraud, hijacking, illegal gambling, loansharking, money laundering, murder, pier thefts, pornography, prostitution, racketeering, and waste management violations. This family covered up with good deeds. So many make me feel good deeds without Christ and purity is being encouraged. Remember God will judge everything we do, including every secret thing, whether good or bad (Ecclesiastes 12:14)

CHEW ON THIS: You should seek to live pure lives because to do so glorifies God. Not simply morality, being nice, etc. But pleasing God because you love Him and want to honor Him.

CONCLUSION
Doing well is one of the things we got from Jesus as His creation and followers. To be of a good deed in the sight of God, it must be thoughts, words or actions that conform to God's law (Deuteronomy 5:32). ***God's law is the only standard of good deeds. It is not the ways of society at a certain time.***

CLOSE IN PRAYER!!

WEEKLY QUIET TIME

DAY	BIBLE PASSAGE	SHARE YOUR DISCOVERIES BELOW
Monday	Ephesians 2:10	
Tuesday	1 John 2:17	
Wednesday	Ecclesiastes 12:13-14	
Thursday	Matthew 7:21-23	
Friday	Ecclesiastes 9:10	
Saturday	Ecclesiastes 3:1	

LESSON 24
SECOND INTERACTIVE SESSION AND QUIZ 2

Dear Teachers,

Please note the following:
- Make the interactive session interesting.
- Ensure the teens participate by allowing them to contribute and state what they have learned as well as ask questions.
- Prepare your own questions and quiz that you will ask them based on the previous lessons.
- You may award gifts to those who perform well in the quiz.
- Create an avenue for the teens to give useful suggestions on how the Sunday School Class can be improved.

Below are some suggested questions you can ask – feel free to add to them!
- Mention five or more previous lesson topics.
- Ask if they remember the Bible passages of each lesson.
- Ask them to recite the memory verses.
- Ask questions from the Activities session as well.
- Ask them questions on the body of the lessons.

WEEKLY QUIET TIME

DAY	BIBLE PASSAGE	SHARE YOUR DISCOVERIES BELOW
Monday	Ruth 2: 1-3	
Tuesday	Ruth 2: 4-7	
Wednesday	Ruth 2: 8-13	
Thursday	Ruth 2: 14-16	
Friday	Ruth 2: 17-19	
Saturday	Ruth 2: 20-23	

LESSON 25
CAN YOU GUESS?

BIBLE READING
Psalm 139: 1-10

MEMORY VERSE
"He did not need any testimony about man, for He knew what was in a man" John 2:25

MAIN POINT: Nothing is hidden from God!

INTRODUCTION
Have you ever tried to hide something from your friends, parents and even God? Interestingly, each of us at one time in our lives or the other have tried to hide something from God. Adam and Eve tried this in Garden of Eden; but why do we do this knowing that God is All Knowing. He even knows your thought and words before the come out of your mouth, but we try to hide from Him even in prayer. He knows everything about you; and yes, He still loves you!

CLASS ACTIVITY
Ice Breaker: What is the first thing you notice when meeting new people?

Game Description: You need to guess the key events in another person's life?

Instructions:
- Divide the group into two and have the youth pair up with someone they are not close to.
- In each pair, they will take turns suggesting the most exciting and memorable experiences of another person's life. At least five points! Keep this to only positive descriptions or experiences.
- Partners must then explain to each other which guesses were accurate and which were incorrect.
- Allow a few minutes for partners to describe some of the true events in their lives that were not guessed.

LESSON 25
CAN YOU GUESS?

- After partners have guessed and responded, have them take turns introducing each other to the entire group. Share one truth you just learned about the other person in your introduction.

CLASS DISCUSSION
- What were some of the key events that have helped your life?
- How did these events make you the person you are today?
- What key negative feelings are you holding on to?
- Are you living in past mistakes and hurt or using them as learning experiences to move forward into a new future?
- What is a key decision you need to make today that could affect your future?
- What is one LESSON you recently learned that you need to act upon to seize the opportunities ahead of you?

ACTION: This week, make it a point to tell at least one person about the difference Jesus has made in your life. (John 4:29)

CONCLUSION
And we know [with great confidence] that God [who is deeply concerned about us] causes all things to work together [as a plan] for good for those who love God, to those who are called according to His plan and purpose. Romans 8:28 Amplified.

WEEKLY QUIET TIME

DAY	BIBLE PASSAGE	SHARE YOUR DISCOVERIES BELOW
Monday	1 Corinthians 1:9	
Tuesday	Romans 8:35-39	
Wednesday	Romans 5:3-4	
Thursday	Genesis 50:20	
Friday	Romans 8:28	
Saturday	Romans 5:8	

THE ZEAL FOR TEENS | 2023/2024

LESSON 26
REWIND IT!

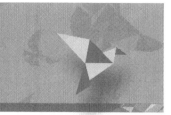

BIBLE READING

Genesis 18:14

MEMORY VERSE

"For with God nothing shall be impossible" Luke 1:37

MAIN POINT: Every moment is an opportunity; be grateful!

INTRODUCTION
"Keep on asking, and you will receive what you ask for. Keep on seeking, and you will find. Keep on knocking, and the door will be opened to you.

CLASS DISCUSSION

Damar Hamlin
On January 2, 2023, twenty-four-year-old Damar Hamlin suffered a cardiac arrest while playing for the Buffalo Bills on a Monday night. Hamlin was given emergency assistance before being taken to the hospital.

Players from the Bills and their opponents, the Cincinnati Bengals, prayed on the field. Those watching the event reacted with shock, horror, and sadness, with many commentators offering prayers of their own. Social Media was bombarded with prayers and the rest of the game was postponed.

For fans at home, the very real fragility of our mortal lives collided with what was supposed to be an exciting and entertaining game. For some, it was a lot to process.

Discussion of what happened to Hamlin as well as speculation on his recovery remain a focus of conversation for weeks following the event THANK GOD FOR ANSWERING PRAYERS!

LESSON 26
REWIND IT!

Discuss the following questions:
- In Hamlin's moment of need, it seems like many people were compelled to pray in that moment. Why do you think that might be?
- Why and when should we pray? Psalm 34:4
- Why do we ignore praying and only seek God when our backs are against the wall?
- Do you pray daily or just when you need something?
- Was it shocking to see Hamlin's collapse on the field? Why or why not?
- What do you think of the decision to postpone the game?

ACTION: Write it down in your own words: 1 Thessalonians 5:17-19

_____
_____
_____
_____

Teachers' Corner: Can we all agree together to have days of Prayer; when we intentionally seek God every day through prayer and fasting as we ask Him to move in and through us in powerful ways.

CLOSE IN PRAYER!!

WEEKLY QUIET TIME

DAY	BIBLE PASSAGE	SHARE YOUR DISCOVERIES BELOW
Monday	Psalm 46:1-3	
Tuesday	Psalm 55:22	
Wednesday	Psalm 91:1-2	
Thursday	1 Peter 5:7	
Friday	Romans 8:28	
Saturday	Psalm 100	

WHAT IT MEANS TO "FEAR NOT"

Fear is a natural response to challenges or the unknown. It's an emotion that serves a valuable purpose – think fight or flight response – but it can quickly become unhealthy when it paralyzes us or propels us into a frantic behavior. Negative outcomes aside, the Bible actually commands us to not be afraid. In fact, there are over 300 variations of the command to "fear not" throughout Scripture.

As Christians, we don't need to fear because we know God is in control. God is on His throne, meaning nothing else is – not even a diagnosis, unmet expectations, or uncertain future. He alone has all power and all authority, and nothing can threaten that.

That means when fear creeps in, we believers are called to take our fear and sift it through the unfailing promises of God and His unchanging character.

Memorizing Scripture is a powerful tool in the fight against fear. The Bible tells us that we have everything we need for life and godliness (2 Peter 1:3) and renewing our minds through the living Word of God is proof of that. Some Bible verses on Fear to memorize: Isaiah 41:10, Hebrews 13:5b-6, Psalm 23:4, Deuteronomy 31:6, John 14:27, Psalm 27:1.

Just for Fun!
An app called RetroPod makes your phone look like an old school iPod. The app draws in titles from your Apple Music library and lets you scroll through them via a "wheel" the way you would back before smartphones became ubiquitous. Interestingly, the app has been gaining a lot of visibility on TikTok, where presumably many users are too young to have had an iPod to begin with. For now, that app seems like one of the more harmless TikTok trends as teens engage with the classic interface like it's 2003.

LESSON 27
JUSTIFICATION & SANCTIFICATION

 MAIN POINT: We are justified by our faith and sanctified by the Word.

INTRODUCTION:
Our justification was secured by Jesus' sacrifice on the cross, none of us could have earned it, so we can be assured that no one can condemn us: "There is therefore now no condemnation to them which are in Christ Jesus, who walk not after the flesh, but after the Spirit" Romans 8:1. Rejoice in the finished work of Jesus!

CLASS DISCUSSION
- **What is justification?** Justification is being considered righteous before God, where the sins of the sinner are no longer remembered by God. It is because of justification that we enjoy peace with God (Romans 5:1; and 2 Corinthians 5:17). Justification is God's act of removing the guilt and penalty of sin while at the same time declaring a sinner righteous through Christ's atoning sacrifice.

    - How can you receive justification?
        - We receive this justification by _____ (Romans 3:25-26).
        - We receive it by His _____ (Titus 3:4-7; Romans 4:5).

- **What is sanctification?** Sanctification is the process of being set apart for God's work and being conformed to the image of Christ.
    - Conformity to Christ involves the work of the person, but it is still God working in the

BIBLE READING
Romans 5:1-5

MEMORY VERSE
"That having been justified by His grace we should become heirs according to the hope of eternal life." Titus 3:7 (NKJV)

LESSON 27
JUSTIFICATION & SANCTIFICATION

    believer to produce more of a godly character in the person who has already been justified (Phil. 2:13).
- Sanctification is not instantaneous because it is not the work of God alone. The justified person is actively involved in submitting to God's will, resisting sin, seeking holiness, and working to be godlier; Galatians 5:22-23; 2 Timothy 2:21; John 17:1-26.
- What role does God's Word play in sanctification?
- What is your role in sanctification?
- We are sanctified by the _____ John 17:17; Ephesians 5:26.

- Understanding to differentiate between Justification and Sanctification is very important to our salvation and growing into maturity in Christ Jesus.
    - Justification is distinct from sanctification because in justification God does not make the sinner righteous; He declares that person righteous (Romans 3:28; Galatians 2:16).
    - Justification deposits Christ's righteousness to the sinner's account (Romans 4:11b); sanctification imparts righteousness to the sinner personally and practically (Romans 6:1-7; 8:11-14).
    - Justification takes place outside sinners and changes their standing (Romans 5:1-2), sanctification is internal and changes the believer's state (Romans 6:19).

CONCLUSION
Justification is an event, sanctification a process.

CLOSE IN PRAYER!!

WEEKLY QUIET TIME

DAY	BIBLE PASSAGE	SHARE YOUR DISCOVERIES BELOW
Monday	1 Samuel 3:1-19	
Tuesday	1 Timothy 5:17-25	
Wednesday	Hebrews 2:1-4	
Thursday	Psalm 66:13-20	
Friday	Nehemiah 9:5-7	
Saturday	1 Chronicles 13: 1-14	

LESSON 28
BAPTISM

RCCG, NORTH AMERICA

 MAIN POINT: Be baptized and be filled with the Holy Ghost.

INTRODUCTION
What does baptism do? As we'll see, Christ not only commands believers to get baptized, but baptism is also a gift he graciously gives for our benefit and blessing.

CLASS DISCUSSION
- **Water Baptism:** Water baptism is a symbol of Jesus Christ's death, burial, and resurrection. We enter the water as a symbol of entering into a relationship with Jesus Christ, coming just as we are, clothed in our old life with all of its habits, mindsets and behaviors. It serves as an outward sign and testimony of an inward grace. The believer has been crucified with Christ, buried with Him, and raised together with Him to walk in newness of life; Galatians 2:20; Romans 6:4.
    - Three reasons to get baptized:
        - Obedience to Christ's command
        - Publicly profess faith in Christ
        - Formally commit yourself to Christ and His people.

    - The process of water baptism:
        - It is done after repenting from sin and receiving salvation in Christ; Mark 16:16
        - It should be done by immersion; Matthew 3:11-17
        - The water baptism should be done in the name of the name of _____; Matthew 28:19

BIBLE READING

Matthew 3:13-17, Acts 2:1-4

MEMORY VERSE

"And so it is with prayer—keep on asking and you will keep on getting; keep on looking and you will keep on finding; knock and the door will be opened." Luke 11:9

LESSON 28
BAPTISM

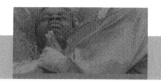

- The purpose of water baptism:
  1. _____
  2. To show that a new believer has been joined with Christ in His death, burial, and resurrection.
  3. Why should we be baptized? _____; Matthew 28.19.

Remember: Christians should be baptized out of obedience to and love for our Lord Jesus.

- **Holy Spirit Baptism:** It is the promise of God to all the believers!
  - Discuss the following questions and support answers with Scriptures:
    - How do I receive the baptism of the Holy Spirit?
    - What does the Holy Spirit do in and for us?
    - What did Jesus tell us about the Holy Spirit?
    - What happens after the Baptism of the Holy Spirit?
    - What is this Scripture saying to us? Romans 8:9

Read Acts 5:32; Acts 8:14-17, Acts 2:38-39!

ACTION: Ask for the power of the Holy Spirit today.

CONCLUSION
Water baptism along with the Holy Spirit baptism is part of the Christian experience. When we receive Jesus by faith, we begin an immediate personal relationship with God. The Holy Spirit works in us to help us become like Christ.

CLOSE IN PRAYER!!

WEEKLY QUIET TIME

DAY	BIBLE PASSAGE	SHARE YOUR DISCOVERIES BELOW
Monday	Acts 10:44-46	
Tuesday	Acts 11:15	
Wednesday	Acts 8:12-17	
Thursday	Luke 24:49	
Friday	Acts 1:4-5	
Saturday	Acts 1:6-11	

LESSON 29
WHAT MAKES AN ENGAGING WITNESS?

 MAIN POINT: Share the gospel or point people to Jesus Christ.

INTRODUCTION
Move your teenagers off the couch and out of the sit-down class and discussion mode, and instead consciously plan an outreach that helps them shine like the brightest star in the sky.

CLASS DISCUSSION
Someone's email to us reads: "If your God exists, I wonder if he would care about me. I've done some pretty stupid stuff in my life. My thoughts are that he would look my way in disdain and complete and utter disappointment."

- Does this email resonate with you? Why or why not?
- What characteristics does a person need to share their faith in genuine and authentic ways?
- What does the Bible say about evangelism?
- How can we develop confidence in our own faith beliefs?
- How do we bring Jesus to more people?
- How can you successfully start spiritual conversations with people?
- What should I say to start a conversation?
- How do I talk with close friends, family members; without risking relationship you don't want to risk! 1 Cor 9:20-22.
- Why should we win souls? John 5:24
- What are some hindrances to soul winning? _____;
  2 Timothy 2:15
- Fear of others; Acts 1:8

BIBLE READING

Romans 2: 1-10

MEMORY VERSE

"Truly, truly, I say to you, whoever hears my word and believes him who sent me has eternal life. He does not come into judgment but has passed from death to life." John 5:24

LESSON 29
WHAT MAKES AN ENGAGING WITNESS?

- _____ ask for boldness (Romans 1:16).
- When you think you are too young to witness.
- Fear of rejection.

CONCLUSION
There are many examples of evangelism in the Bible, with Jesus Himself being the greatest evangelist of all. Perhaps, the most well-known Bible verse about evangelism comes from Mark 16:15-16 — "And he said to them, 'Go into all the world and proclaim the gospel to the whole creation. Whoever believes and is baptized will be saved, but whoever does not believe will be condemned."

ACTION: Do I really know where I am in my spiritual journey? And how am I modeling faith to my friends?

Below are a few Youth Church Outreach Ideas! Please consider doing a youth group outreach sometime this year!
- Volunteer at a Senior Center.
- Volunteer at a Homeless Shelter.
- Feed the Homeless on the Streets.
- Run Errands for Elderly and Disabled People.
- Organize a Tech Support Day.
- Visit Patients in a Hospital.
- Tutor Younger Students.

Teacher's Corner:
Designate an "Ice Cream Outreach Month" where you challenge every Christian in your group to treat one unreached friend to ice cream one-on-one – with the aim of using the time to initiate a faith-sharing conversation. Then close out your month with a youth group ice cream social that students can invite their friends to – and give the gospel.
Volunteer your group at a homeless shelter, community center, etc. If you want to give students an opportunity to directly interact with those in need, organize a time to volunteer at a homeless shelter, community center, or other local organization where students can serve others. This is actually a great event for the cooler weather because many of these

LESSON 29
WHAT MAKES AN ENGAGING WITNESS?

organizations need help indoors. Again, students should be prepared to have Gospel conversations with those they meet, but it's also important to respect the guidelines of the organization you're working with. Check out Dare.2 share.com!

CLOSE IN PRAYER!!

WEEKLY QUIET TIME

DAY	BIBLE PASSAGE	SHARE YOUR DISCOVERIES BELOW
Monday	2 Timothy 4:5	
Tuesday	1 Peter 3:15	
Wednesday	2 Corinthians 5:20	
Thursday	1 Corinthians 1:17	
Friday	John 5:24	
Saturday	2 Timothy 4:22	

LESSON 30
REVIEW 3

TAKE A STEP BACK & REWIND

It is time to review the lessons 25 - 29.
- Ask your teacher about the topics you don't understand.
- Be ready to participate and answer the questions for discussion.

CLASS DISCUSSION
- What would you say to a friend who wants to know about your Christian faith?
- Can you explain the topic that challenges you the most?
- What did you learn from the previous lessons?
- Name two topics from the previous lessons.
- Please share the most significant change you've experienced based on previous chapters.
- Feel free to ask questions for more clarity on any of the previous lessons.

Teacher's Corner: The youths will need a notebook and pen for next week's lesson, please ask your youths to prepare accordingly.

WEEKLY QUIET TIME

DAY	BIBLE PASSAGE	SHARE YOUR DISCOVERIES BELOW
Monday	Ruth 3: 1-5	
Tuesday	Ruth 3: 6-8	
Wednesday	Ruth 3: 9-13	
Thursday	Ruth 3: 14-18	
Friday	1 Samuel 17:12	
Saturday	Matthew 1:5	

LESSON 31
TEN-YEAR PLAN!

 MAIN POINT: As believers, we don't live by chance but by purpose.

INTRODUCTION
Living in the fullness of God's purpose for our lives, requires us to deliberately seek direction from God and follow His directions. This requires planning ahead and entrusting our future into God's hands. "A goal without a plan is just a wish" - Antoine de Saint-Exupéry!

CLASS DISCUSSION
- How can a teenager prepare for the future?
- What should I do in my teenage years?
- What life skills do I need before I leave home?
- What is my priority right now?
- Focus on goals that are SMART: specific, measurable, achievable, relevant, and time-based.

ACTIVITY BELOW AFTER READING THE STORY
READ THE STORY: When I was a junior in high school, I went to a Christian retreat, and one of the speakers had filled this out. ***I think it was a ten-year plan.*** He had us put where we saw ourselves and where we wanted to see ourselves ten years in the future. So, something that I thought I wanted to see was having a degree and great career. Secondly: getting married to a godly man who was a spiritual leader and who loved Jesus more than he loved me. I wanted to see myself as a young lady who had wisdom and who loved the Lord. That was where I wanted to see myself in ten years, so he said next, ***"Take it back five years***, what do you have to do in the next five years to get there in ten years?"* I then wrote down that, well, it

BIBLE READING

Habakkuk 2:2-3

MEMORY VERSE

"I will instruct thee and teach thee in the way which thou shalt go: I will guide thee with mine eye." Psalm 32:8

LESSON 31
TEN-YEAR PLAN!

looks like I need to be focused on my education and making myself a godly woman who that Godly man would be attracted to. It starts with me becoming that Godly woman and gaining that wisdom over time through God and God's Word.

And then he asked, **'What do you need to do in the next two years to get there?'** So then, I'm thinking, alright, well, it kind of starts with making sure I'm reading my Bible every day, that I'm taking theology and just growing in my faith. He asked, **"What do you need to do in the next six months to get there?"**

Suddenly, it just made me realize that everything that I'm doing right now affects what my life looks like in 10 years and that there's no time to waste. **Therefore, if there's one thing, I can give you advice on, is to know how you act.**

CLASS ACTIVITY (MY TEN-YEAR PLAN)
You are going to start working on your ten-year plan in class, if not done by the end of class, please can finish it at home!
Grab a notebook and a pen; make sure you give your imagination room to roam. Here are the basic steps you should take to create your plan (don't forget to ask for help if needed!):
- Consider what you want for your life.
- Write down your dream or Vision!
- List your current skills (include educational skills/degrees)
- Write down your educational goals.
- Identify your challenges and help needed to overcome.
- Learn more about your goal(s) and what will be needed to achieve it.
- Refine your goals.
- Write down your immediate next steps.
- Be prepared for changes!

CLOSE IN PRAYER!!

Teacher's Corner: The following are some recommended books you may want to share with your youths: (1) The 7 Habits of Highly Effective

LESSON 31
TEN-YEAR PLAN!

Teens by Sean Covey; (2) Smile & Succeed for Teens: A Crash Course in Face-to-Face Communication; (3) Parent's Guide for Smile & Succeed for Teens: Job Skills and Social Skills for Teens.

WEEKLY QUIET TIME

DAY	BIBLE PASSAGE	SHARE YOUR DISCOVERIES BELOW
Monday	James 4:13-17	
Tuesday	Jeremiah 29:11	
Wednesday	Philippians 1:6	
Thursday	James 1:5	
Friday	Proverbs 27:12	
Saturday	Philippians 4:6	

THE ZEAL FOR TEENS | 2023/2024

LESSON 32 (ACTIVITY)
BEHIND THE NAME

BIBLE READING

Psalms 139:14-18

MEMORY VERSE

"And the Lord said to Moses, "I will do the very thing you have asked, because I am pleased with you, and I know you by name". Exodus 33:17

MAIN POINT: Use this icebreaker to learn about the names of people in your group.

INTRODUCTION

Everyone has stories, often fascinating ones, based around their Names. Whatever your name, always remember God knows you by name and loves you. He has a plan for your life and your future if you will trust Him.

CLASS ACTIVITY

Instructions: Divide participants into groups of three to five people and have each person in the group take a turn — telling the story of his/her name. Group members can share as much or as little information as they like. Use the following questions as a guide:

- Where does your name come from?
- Do you like your name? Why or why not?
- Do you know the meaning of your name? Explain?
- How did you get your name?
- Why did your parents give you your first name or middle name?
- Do you have any pet names / cute names your family or friends call you?
- What nicknames have people given to you?
- What's the story of your last name/ family name?
- Where did it come from?
- What do you know about your family name?
- How far can you trace back your family tree?
- What are some interesting people and events in your family history?

LESSON 32 (ACTIVITY)
BEHIND THE NAME

CLASS DISCUSSION
Each group should share the most interesting story they heard in their group!

While your family name can tell you a lot about your past, your future is determined by your choices.
- What type of legacy would you like to leave behind?
- To get that reputation and or legacy, what are the things would you need to do?
- How can you begin moving from where you are now in life to a point where people will remember you by the legacy you desire to leave behind?

Make It Spiritual
- Can you relate with the Scripture verse in Isaiah 43:1-3 & Isaiah 49:16?
- God knew Moses by name; *Exodus 33:17*.
- God called Jeremiah before he was even born; *Jeremiah 1:5*.
- What does Psalms 139:14-18 tell us?
- Jesus calls us each by name and guides us; *John 10:3*.
- Are you amazed by Matthew 10:24-33? *Luke 10:17-20*.

ACTION: If there is one thing, I wish you would get out of this TOPIC; is that you're encouraged toward greater freedom and confidence in Christ. God never stops pursuing you and redirecting you toward His plan. Remember, it is His calling on your life, so He is faithful in helping you accomplish it. What is something you can begin doing today to leave behind a legacy for your family name?

CONCLUSION: We serve a merciful, loving, and generous God who has chosen us. He has a plan for us, and we can trust Him with it. Throughout the Bible God called people by name. Sometimes he even changed the name of people in the Bible to reflect their character and reinforce the decisions they made in following Him.

Used with permission by Ken Sapp and Joshua Goh

LESSON 32 (ACTIVITY)
BEHIND THE NAME

CLOSE IN PRAYER!!

📖 WEEKLY QUIET TIME

DAY	BIBLE PASSAGE	SHARE YOUR DISCOVERIES BELOW
Monday	Genesis 22:14	
Tuesday	Exodus 15:26	
Wednesday	Exodus 3:14	
Thursday	Genesis 17:1	
Friday	Judges 6:24	
Saturday	Exodus 48:35	

LESSON 33
ONE THING!

 MAIN POINT: What is that one thing you need to focus on as Christian!

INTRODUCTION
As Christians, how can we make sense of our world, our relationships and our faith without the knowledge and understanding of the Bible? All entangling things must be given up.

CLASS DISCUSSION
Read and discuss Luke 10:38-42.
- How can I apply what I have learnt to/in my life?
- What is the one thing that Martha did?
- Why is it so important?
- Do I need a change in attitude?
- Are there actions to take or leave entirely?
- Is there an example to follow?
- Do I need to confess something to God?

Read Ecclesiastes 12:1-7
- In our daily lives, what place does God really have?
  _____

- What advice was given to you from the Bible passage above?
  _____

- What is the first thing to seek in life? Matthew 6:33
  _____

- What makes it difficult to live as a Christian at home?
  _____

- What makes it difficult to live as a Christian at school?
  _____

BIBLE READING

Luke 10:38-42

MEMORY VERSE

"There is only one thing worth being concerned about. Mary has discovered it, and it will not be taken away from her". Luke 10:42

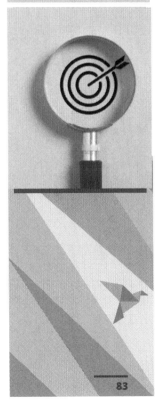

LESSON 33
ONE THING!

ACTION: John 14: 26; 1 John 2: 27. I challenge you to read the Bible on your own, not just read with others in the Youth Group, or during Bible Study Sessions, but on your own. No one would be ringing a bell or setting an alert for you. The challenge is for you to take the initiative yourself.

CONCLUSION
In a time when biblical illiteracy is trending very high, when most church-going youths have settled into a mushy, uninformed, "build-your-own-as-you-go" approach to Christianity, with no interest in the Word of God, you should seek the things of God and prioritize it over the things of the world.

CLOSE IN PRAYER!!

WEEKLY QUIET TIME

DAY	BIBLE PASSAGE	SHARE YOUR DISCOVERIES BELOW
Monday	Matthew 6:33	
Tuesday	2 Timothy 3:16	
Wednesday	Acts 2:38	
Thursday	Hebrews 3:12-19	
Friday	1 John 2:6	
Saturday	Galatians 2:20	

LESSON 34
DON'T MISS OUT!

 MAIN POINT: If we take in God's Word, we will receive the grace to overcome any difficulty that arises in our lives.

BIBLE READING

Psalm 19: 7-11

INTRODUCTION
The Word of God is food for our spirit. Some believers don't seem to realize that we really do need to feed our spirit, similarly to how we need to feed our physical bodies. There are too many believers that are basically "spiritually anemic" – weak, unreliable, easily and easily defeated.

MEMORY VERSE

"Your word is a lamp to guide my feet and a light for my path." Psalm 119:105

CLASS DISCUSSION
Discuss how the Bible helps you in every situation life can throw at you!
- Do you want to overcome doubts, fear, and anxiety? The Bible helps us defeat them by strengthening our faith; *Romans 10:17.*
- Do you desire to defeat the presence of sin in your life? The Bible helps us fight sin in our lives; *John 17:17.*
- Do you struggle with important and difficult decisions? The Bible helps us to make decisions according to His will so that He will bless us.
  - The Bible also increases your wisdom in every area of your life. *Proverbs 1-4.*
  - The Bible gives you clear guidance and direction for much of your life. Psalm 119:105.
- Are you having a difficulty finding good friends? Read *Proverbs 14:7; Proverbs 22:24; and 1 Corinthians 15:33.*
- Do you feel weak against the crafty schemes of the devil? *James 4:7 & Ephesians 6:11.*

LESSON 34
DON'T MISS OUT!

- The Bible tells you how to be genuinely saved and how to grow up in your faith; *John 3:16; Romans 12:1-2.*
- How do you detect truth from falsehood? The Bible helps us to detect falsehood in a world filled with lies. 1 John 5:19 & Ephesians 6:14.
  - The Bible empowers your prayer life. Philippians 4:6-7.
  - The Bible sharpens your ability to hear the voice of the Holy Spirit more clearly in your life. 1 Corinthians 1:5.
- Have you ever wanted to encourage someone when they are hurting or discouraged? The Bible is powerful enough to revive the soul! Psalm 19:7.

ACTION: How can I apply what I have learned to my life? Things we should seek to do with the Word of God every day; (1) Read it! (2) Hear it! (3) Believe it! (4) Speak it! (5) Obey it! (6) Pray it! (7) Meditate on it!

REALITY CHECK: Do I need a change in attitude? Are there actions to take or avoid?

CONCLUSION
True Christian faith transforms our conduct as well as our thoughts.

CLOSE IN PRAYER!!

WEEKLY QUIET TIME

DAY	BIBLE PASSAGE	SHARE YOUR DISCOVERIES BELOW
Monday	1 Peter 5:8	
Tuesday	James 4:7	
Wednesday	1 John 3:8	
Thursday	Ephesians 6:12	
Friday	John 8:44	
Saturday	2 Timothy 3:16 - 17	

LESSON 35
WHO IS YOUR MENTOR?

 MAIN POINT: A good mentor will influence you positively.

BIBLE READING

Proverbs 1:8-9

INTRODUCTION
The role of a mentor in one's life is important. Elijah helped Elisha to become great. We also need someone who is more experienced and respected that will help us achieve our goals in life.

MEMORY VERSE

"As iron sharpens iron, so a friend sharpens a friend" Proverbs 27:17

CLASS DISCUSSION
- Who is a mentor? A mentor is a wise and trusted counselor, parent or teacher. 1 Kings 19:19-21.
- Why do we need a mentor?
  - ▪ _____
  - ▪ We need someone to help re-shape our character to succeed in life.
  - ▪ We _____ need
  - ▪ To avoid mistake that may hinder your lives.
- Who can be our mentor?
  - ▪ Our _____ (Proverbs 1:8-9).
  - ▪ Our _____ (Proverbs 5:13).
  - ▪ Our _____ (Support with Scripture).
- What should be our attitude toward our mentor?
- What is the difference between a mentor and a counselor?
  _____
- Tips for Finding and Working with a Mentor:
  - ▪ o Choose a mentor whose values are like your own.
  - ▪ o Your mentor should have time to build the relationship.

LESSON 35
WHO IS YOUR MENTOR?

- Take the initial step in establishing contact with a potential mentor since you are the one who will benefit the most from the relationship.
- Parents, Ministers, or leaders with good character (2 Timothy 2:24).
- Matured and good personality.
- Work with your mentor to accomplish specific goals.
- Establish mutual trust and respect.

- **Lessons in Mentorship:** The story of Elijah and Elisha may be the most obvious mentorship story in the Bible. It tells us much about both the role of the protégé and the mentor. Other examples of mentorship in the Bible include:
    - Jesus and His _____?
    - Eli and _____?
    - Moses and _____?
    - Paul and _____?

CHEW ON THIS: We must be vigilant and watchful to avoid dealing with a predator rather than a mentor (1 Peter 5:8).

ACTION: Growing mentally and socially comes from learning, listening and obeying instructions and teaching. God the Father, God the Son and the God the Holy Spirit [The Holy Trinity] is the perfect and best Mentor, they can never fail or mislead you. Ask Him today to mentor you!

CLOSE IN PRAYER!

WEEKLY QUIET TIME

DAY	BIBLE PASSAGE	SHARE YOUR DISCOVERIES BELOW
Monday	Matthew 28:20	
Tuesday	Proverbs 22:6	
Wednesday	Titus 2: 3-4	
Thursday	Psalm 71:18	
Friday	Proverbs 27:17	
Saturday	2 Kings 4:38-41	

LESSON 36
"IN CHRIST"

💡 **MAIN POINT:** Do you believe this statement: You can only truly know who you are by truly knowing God?

INTRODUCTION
A person can shape circumstances, but circumstances should never be allowed to shape a person. We should master circumstances, not the other way around.

CLASS DISCUSSION
- What does it mean to be "in Christ?"
- What exactly does it mean to be new?
- What "old thing" would you like to get rid of that impairs your relationship with God?
- Does anyone have any experience what this verse is saying and can they help by sharing their experience?
- Is there any cost to become a new person in Christ?
- What is something about God you do not understand?
- Why is it so difficult to give up things that are not good for us?

REALITY CHECK:
- In the struggle to become "new," it is important to know that we can actually make choices that will help us become "new" creations in Christ.
- Christ can make us new, but as long as we keep holding on to things in our lives that drag us down, He cannot take them away from us.

BIBLE READING

2 Corinthians 4: 1-6

MEMORY VERSE

"This means that anyone who belongs to Christ has become a new person. The old life is gone; a new life has begun! 2 Corinthians 5:17 (NLT)

LESSON 36
"IN CHRIST"

- The true evidence that you are truly a "new creation" is that you live your life for Jesus Christ and not yourself.

CONCLUSION

A New Creation Means a New Person, Perspective and a New Purpose.

CLOSE IN PRAYER!!

DAY	BIBLE PASSAGE	SHARE YOUR DISCOVERIES BELOW
Monday	2 Corinthians 4: 1-6	
Tuesday	2 Corinthians 5:17	
Wednesday	Psalm 2	
Thursday	1 Corinthians 1:1-9	
Friday	1 Corinthians 1:10-17	
Saturday	1 Corinthians 1: 18-25	

LESSON 37 (ACTIVITY)
TEAMWORK

 MAIN POINT: Everyone has a role to play in the journey of life; do your part!

INTRODUCTION
Don't hit back; discover beauty in everyone. If you've got it in you, get along with everybody. Don't insist on getting even; that's not for you to do. "I'll do the judging," says God. "I'll take care of it." Romans 12:17-19 (MSG)

CLASS ACTIVITY *(The Back-To-Back Get Up)*
The game begins with two players sitting back-to-back with their arms hooked together, with their feet flat on the floor in front of them, and legs should be together. The goal of this game is for the players to stand up together without using any hands.

As soon as this is accomplished, add another player to hook arms with the other two players and to go from sitting to standing. Keep adding a new person each time until the entire group successfully stands up.

Materials needed: None, just space enough to keep adding new players to the group!

CHEW ON THIS: Getting up from this seating position – feet flat on the floor and legs together – is usually difficult to do by yourself without using your hands – throw your hands up! – but having someone else to support you made a lot easier. Things always work better with teamwork and a positive attitude; the Bible says two is better than one (Eccl. 4:9)

BIBLE READING

Mark 6:7-13

MEMORY VERSE

"We love because he first loved us." 1 John 4:19

LESSON 37 (ACTIVITY)
TEAMWORK

CLASS DISCUSSION

Read: 1 Corinthians 12:12–27 - Calls us to be one body with many different parts. It reminds us that togetherness is oneness, not sameness.
- What does the Bible teach about teamwork?
- Why is unity so important to God?
- Can team work succeed without unity?
- If we are to maintain the unity the Spirit has given us; we must cultivate the same qualities found in our Lord Jesus.
- In Ephesians 4:2-3, Paul highlights five of these qualities:
    1. _____
    2. _____
    3. _____
    4. _____
    5. _____
- How did Jesus demonstrate teamwork? *Mark 6:7-13*
- How can we apply this Bible passage to our lives? *Ephesians 4:15-16*
- How can we come together and demonstrate the love of Christ at home?

REALITY CHECK: You can beat the odds; you can keep your Family Together! How? By leading them to God, teaching them about God, and keeping them near God.

ACTION: What's one thing that would be difficult for you to give up about yourself to improve yourself if you gave it away right now?

CLOSE IN PRAYER!!

WEEKLY QUIET TIME

DAY	BIBLE PASSAGE	SHARE YOUR DISCOVERIES BELOW
Monday	James 2:18	
Tuesday	John 3:16	
Wednesday	John 14:6	
Thursday	1 John 4:19	
Friday	Romans 5:8	
Saturday	James 2:19-20	

ON YOUR OWN (OYO): JUST FOR FUN!

Answer the following trivia questions:

1. Q: Which eyelid-less animal licks its eyeballs to keep them moist?
   A: _____
2. Q: Which famous author taste-tested Cadbury chocolates as a schoolboy?
   A: _____
3. Q: Which US state quarter features magnolia blossoms?
   A: _____
4. Q: What is the square root of 2025?
   A: _____
5. Q: Which popular sitcom was originally called "Insomnia Cafe" before airing?
   A: _____

LESSON 38
THIRD INTERACTIVE SESSION AND QUIZ 3

Dear Teachers,

Please note the following:
- Make the interactive session interesting.
- Ensure the teens participate by allowing them to contribute and state what they have learned as well as ask questions.
- Prepare your own questions and quiz that you will ask them based on the previous lessons.
- You may give gifts to those who perform well in the quiz.
- Create an avenue for the teens to give useful suggestions on how the Sunday School Class can be improved.

Below are some suggested questions you can ask – feel free to add to them!
- Mention five or more previous LESSON TOPICS.
- Ask if they remember the Bible passages of each lesson.
- Ask them to recite the memory verses.
- Ask questions from the Activities session as well.
- Ask them questions on the body of the lessons.

📖 WEEKLY QUIET TIME

DAY	BIBLE PASSAGE	SHARE YOUR DISCOVERIES BELOW
Monday	Ruth 4:1-3	
Tuesday	Ruth 4:4-6	
Wednesday	Ruth 4:7-9	
Thursday	Ruth 4: 10- 12	
Friday	Ruth 4: 13-15	
Saturday	Ruth 4: 16-22	

LESSON 39
WHAT LOVE DOES?

 MAIN POINT: Knowing the truth about love and what love does is liberating.

BIBLE READING
1 Corinthians 13

INTRODUCTION
Love is misunderstood and distorted by the unbelieving world. So, no matter what I say, what I believe, and what I do, I'm bankrupt without love.

MEMORY VERSE
"Most important of all, continue to show deep love for each other, for love covers a multitude of sins." 1 Peter 4:8

CLASS DISCUSSION
- What love is not?
- What does this statement mean to you? "Love is not a feeling but a commitment"?
- What does the Bible teach us about love?
- Are you struggling to receive the love offered to you?
- What does Love do?
- Do a verse-by-verse discussion of 1 Corinthians 13: 1-7
- Based on 1 Corinthians 13: 1-7, can you think of someone with real love for you?
- Sometimes, love can be confusing and how can we love someone we don't agree with?
- In the past five years, can you think of anyone that has given you love?
- Do you have the capacity to love others? John 14:15

REALITY CHECK: You might not be able to always control your feelings; but you are fully in control of your actions. Think about that for a minute!

CHEW ON THIS: "The best math you can learn is to calculate the future cost of your current decisions." Gary Black

LESSON 39
WHAT LOVE DOES?

ACTION: Say thank you to someone who has shown you real love! Show real love to someone today!

CONCLUSION
As we study Paul's description of love in 1 Corinthians 13, it becomes clear that he is not talking about a warm feeling but rather a conscious decision to love other people no matter what. The love Paul is talking about is not primarily something you feel but something you do.

CLOSE IN PRAYER!!

WEEKLY QUIET TIME

DAY	BIBLE PASSAGE	SHARE YOUR DISCOVERIES BELOW
Monday	Philippians 2:3-4	
Tuesday	Mark 10:45	
Wednesday	Proverbs 19:11	
Thursday	Jeremiah 31:34	
Friday	Psalm 130:3-4	
Saturday	1 Corinthians 13:4-7	

LESSON 40
BEHAVIOUR MODIFICATION

 MAIN POINT: Behaviour has rewards and consequences.

INTRODUCTION
Just because something is technically legal doesn't mean that it's spiritually appropriate. If I went around doing whatever I thought I could get by with, I'd be a slave to my whims. Let's face it, we can all use some attitude adjustment or, as experts say, Behaviour Modification.

CLASS DISCUSSION
Read Luke 6: 43-44
- How do you know if someone is a Christian according to these passages?
- Go beyond the surface. Look at your life. How old you are? What are you doing? 1 John 2:4.
- Take all your thoughts and all the words you speak in a day e.g.
  - What you say about your teachers!
  - What you say to your family members!
  - What you say about your family members!
  - What you joke about and what you do in private!
  - What you enjoy watching!
  - What you write in your journal!

Now, describe yourself, based on your thoughts and words? Does anything need to change? 1 John 1:8

REALITY CHECK: What Does My Behaviour Say About Me?

BIBLE READING

1 Corinthians 6:9-11

MEMORY VERSE

"I have the right to do anything," you say—but not everything is beneficial. "I have the right to do anything"— but I will not be mastered by anything." 1 Corinthians 6:12

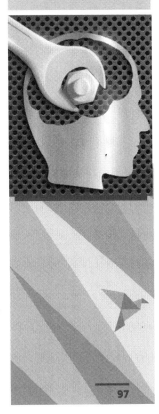

LESSON 40
BEHAVIOUR MODIFICATION

ACTION: Write down the change you want to see, confess, and repent of all known sin!

CONCLUSION
The gospel says real Christians change. This is why unbelievers can legitimately say, "Christians are hypocrites." Isn't your God supposed to change you in some way? The answer is yes. – Jesus is saying, your behaviour will change if you are a believer.

CLOSE IN PRAYER!!

📖 WEEKLY QUIET TIME

DAY	BIBLE PASSAGE	SHARE YOUR DISCOVERIES BELOW
Monday	2 Corinthians 5:6-10	
Tuesday	2 Corinthians 5:11-15	
Wednesday	2 Corinthians 5:16-21	
Thursday	1 Corinthians 6:12-20	
Friday	Matt 7:16-20	
Saturday	Luke 6:43-44	

WHAT DOES THE BIBLE SAY ABOUT THE YOUTH?

Jeremiah 1:4-8 says "Now the word of the Lord came to me, saying, "Before I formed you in the womb, I knew you, and before you were born, I consecrated you; I appointed you a prophet to the nations."

Then I said, "Ah, Lord God! Behold, I do not know how to speak, for I am only a youth." But the Lord said to me, "Do not say, 'I am only a youth'; for to all to whom I send you, you shall go, and whatever I command you, you shall speak. Do not be afraid of them, for I am with you to deliver you, declares the Lord." God made it clear that He can also use the younger generation to do His will and that He will be with them as they obey God.

Aside from this, 1 Timothy 4:12 says that "Let no one despise you for your youth, but set the believers an example in speech, in conduct, in love, in faith, in purity.". This means that the youth should not let anyone despise them for being young as they serve God. Instead, the younger generations should set an example to all followers of Christ in speech, conduct, love, faith, and purity.

THE ZEAL FOR TEENS | 2023/2024

LESSON 41 (ACTIVITY — KARAOKE SUNDAY)
I'M FORGIVEN

BIBLE READING

Psalm 32: 1-5

MEMORY VERSE

"Jesus said, "Father, forgive them, for they do not know what they are doing." And they divided up his clothes by casting lots." Luke 23:34

MAIN POINT: Forgiven people must be forgiving people!

INTRODUCTION

The Bible says in Romans 8:1 there is now no condemnation for those who are in Christ Jesus; it means you are forgiven with NO more guilt. You and I have been set free from the guilt of sin.

CLASS ACTIVITY

Karaoke time! Have students pick any forgiveness contemporary songs and sing and dance to them on YouTube or Spotify. You might even turn this into a "freeze dance" but make it count! (15 Minutes)! In Acts 16:16-34 Paul and Silas sang in prison, so no excuse!

CLASS DISCUSSION

I'm forgiven — What has God done about our problem with sin? Read together out loud (and in order) the references from Romans below.
- Romans 3: 22-26
- Romans 5: 6-11
- Romans 10: 9-10
- Romans 8: 38-39

ASK THE TEACHER: What is the significance of the blood of Jesus for our sins?

REALITY CHECK: If we have put our trust in Christ, we have been completely forgiven. God has promised that he will not remember our sin.

LESSON 41 (ACTIVITY — KARAOKE SUNDAY)
I'M FORGIVEN

But what about the things I still do wrong? How does God see them and what does he do about them? Read 1 John 1: 8-9.

ACTION: Read Psalm 51 and genuinely repent ask God for forgiveness.

CONCLUSION:
The Holy Spirit reminds us where we have failed to live as God wants. Then if we confess, repent – say sorry, turn away, be willing to change – God will keep His promises and we are forgiven and made clean.

CLOSE IN PRAYER!!

WEEKLY QUIET TIME

DAY	BIBLE PASSAGE	SHARE YOUR DISCOVERIES BELOW
Monday	Psalm 51	
Tuesday	Psalm 32	
Wednesday	1 John 1:9	
Thursday	John 8:44	
Friday	Psalm 15	
Saturday	Psalm 16	

LESSON 42
THE MYTH ABOUT FORGIVENESS

BIBLE READING

2 Samuel 12:1-18

MEMORY VERSE

"Behold, to obey is better than sacrifice, and to hearken than the fat of rams" 1 Sam. 15:22

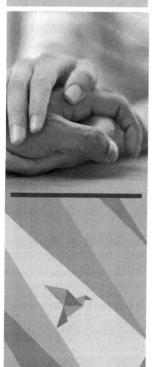

MAIN POINT: Forgiveness does not erase consequences!

INTRODUCTION
The price of David's sin of murder and adultery was high. He spent the rest of his life regretting it.

CLASS DISCUSSION *(Study of the life of David)*
Read 2 Samuel 12:1-18
- What lesson did you learn from David?
- Did God forgive David his sins?
- What was the consequence?
- How did the anger and shame of being called out help David?
- Why did Prophet Nathan not directly accuse David of his sin?
- What was David's reaction to the message from God?
- Does God know every secret about us?
- David reaped what he sowed; was this process true of good things as well as bad?

CHEW ON THIS
- Sin Can Bring Horrible Consequences, but Sin Can Be Forgiven!
- Eli the priest fails to fear God and his two sons are killed because of it.
- Saul fails to obey and honor God, and the kingdom is given to another man.
- • When David takes Bathsheba and kills her husband Uriah, he sins in so many ways, and the Lord is not silent or indifferent to them. In fact, he promises to bring "the sword" upon David's house, and that sword takes four of

LESSON 42
THE MYTH ABOUT FORGIVENESS

his sons. Such sobering consequences for sin are meant to cause us to fear falling into sin.
- David wrote in one Psalm he expressed his mental torment and pleaded for forgiveness. "Create in me a clean heart, O God; and renew a right spirit within me. Cast me not away from thy presence; and take not thy holy spirit from me."; Psalm 51:1-3, 10-11!

REALITY CHECK
- Forgiveness, according to the Bible, is not approving of or diminishing sin!
- Forgiveness is not enabling sin!
- Forgiveness is not denying a wrongdoing!

ACTION: Read over again and pray!
"Then Samuel said, do you think all GOD wants are sacrifices— empty rituals just for show? He wants you to listen to him! Plain listening is the thing, not staging a lavish religious production. Not doing what GOD tells you is far worse than fooling around in the occult. Getting self-important around GOD is far worse than making deals with your dead ancestors. Because you said No to GOD's command, he says No to your kingship."
1 Samuel 15: 22-23 (MSG)

CLOSE IN PRAYER!!

WEEKLY QUIET TIME

DAY	BIBLE PASSAGE	SHARE YOUR DISCOVERIES BELOW
Monday	1 Sam. 15:1-9	
Tuesday	1 Sam. 15:10-23	
Wednesday	1 Sam. 15:22	
Thursday	1 Sam. 15:24-30	
Friday	Psalm 34:1-10	
Saturday	Psalm 74:1	

FOR LEADERS

- Be intentional!
- The teenage church is vital member of the body not to be marginalized at all.
- Youth ministry is challenging and wonderful.
- Teenagers may not have all the answer, but the Church need those vital questions from them.
- Who am I? Important question for us in the youth Church.
- Keep your own Spiritual balance if you want to be an effective leader.
- What are we doing and how? Be prepared for the long haul.
- Calm down on the ever-changing culture and be well informed.
- Relationship matters.
- Read books and attend training!
- Respect is important to your teens and its two-way street.
- Be friendly.
- Discipleship not baby-sitting.
- Partner with parents.
- Develop student leaders.

"A leader is one who knows the way, goes the way, and shows the way." John C. Maxwell

LESSON 43
GOD THE ETERNAL CREATOR (Part 1)

MAIN POINT: There is a difference between knowing about God and knowing Him personally. How can one know this Immortal Being? Is it possible to relate with Him personally? The answer is a resounding yes. God is revealed in creation. His glory is on display all around us. He desires to be known by His children. Though He is infinite, He has made provision for everyone, including young people, to know Him; Ecclesiastes 3:11.

BIBLE READING

Genesis 1:1-5

MEMORY VERSE

"The heavens declare the glory of God; And the firmament shows His handiwork" Psalm 19:1.

INTRODUCTION

God is not a concept or an idea. He is alive and real. All of creation carries the proof of His power and glory; Romans 1:20. His power and glory are beyond debate. The growing denial in the heart of many does not threaten His Sovereignty. He has been, is and will always be God. The area of focus for us is whether we know Him beyond the confusion that the world desires to cast upon our heart. Though it is easy to assume that we know Him, the truth is revealed in our words, actions, and fears. Hence, the question everyone must answer today is, "Do I know God personally and intimately?".

CLASS DISCUSSION
What is there to know?
- His person – Who is this God? What is God's nature and character?
- His Presence – What is His dwelling environment like? What is His requirement for personal interaction? What is the wonder in His majestic presence? How can I attract Him to myself?

LESSON 43
GOD THE ETERNAL CREATOR (Part 1)

- His motives and plans – Why does God do what He does? How does He achieve His purposes?
- His principles (systems, strategies, or wisdom) – What are His methods of operation?
- His Promises – What is His commitment to man?
- His Power – What is His capacity to accomplish His purposes and promises.

What is the nature of this Invisible God?

- **God is Holy** — This is the most important and most emphasized element of His nature; Is. 6:3; Rev. 4:8. He is set apart from all creations. He is incomparable, transcendentally separate, and infinitely above everything else; Is. 40:25, 2 Sam. 7:22, Is. 57:15. Holiness is the foundation of all other aspects of His character; Ps.77:13.
- **God is Triune** — He is one God who has always existed as three distinct Persons: Father, Son, and Holy Spirit; Deut. 6:4; Gen. 1:1, 26; Matt. 3:16-17, Jn. 14:16-17. Each member of the Trinity is God; Heb. 1:8-9.
- **God is Good** — He is good and there is no evil in Him; Ps. 92:15, Jam. 1:13. He glories in goodness (Ex. 33:19). His goodness is in everything that He is and does – His love, His mercy, His kindness, His judgement, His reign; Ps. 69:16, Ps. 119:68.
- **God is Love** — He is the essence of love; 1 Jn. 4:8. The motivation behind His interactions with and the bestowed blessings on mankind is love; Jn 3:16.
- **God is Light** — He is self-revealing in information about Himself; 1 Jn.1:5. He is pure. There is no darkness in Him, and no darkness can hide from Him; Dan. 2:22.
- **God is Sovereign** — He is supreme; Deut. 10:17. All His creations put together cannot thwart His purposes; Ps. 95:3, Jer. 23:20, Eph. 1:11. He is judged by no one and has absolute authority over the entire universe and everything in it; Ps. 115:3. His sovereignty is revealed in His Omni-capacities — Omnipotent, Omniscient and Omnipresent.

LESSON 43
GOD THE ETERNAL CREATOR (Part 1)

- **God is Spirit** — He has a spiritual essence and is invisible to the natural eyes; 1 Tim. 6:16, Jn. 1:18. He has no material body and is by nature intangible yet real and true; Lk. 24:39, Jn. 4:24.
- **God Immortal** — He is eternal, self-existent and self-sufficient; Gen. 17:1, Ex. 3:13-14, 1 Tim. 1:17. He is uncreated and has always existed; Rev. 4:8, Ps. 90:2. He has no beginning and no end; Rev. 1:8.
- **God Immutable** — God does not change; Heb.13:8. He cannot be changed or change Himself; Mal. 3:6, Jam.1:17. He remains the same while everything else is subject to change; Matt. 24:35.
- **God is infinite** — He is perfect and unlimited in all things; Ps. 145:3. He is all there can ever be and beyond; Rev. 1:8. Everything created has a limit, but our Creator is an infinite cut above all creation; Eph. 3:8.

Whenever there is a creation, there must be a creator. Whenever there is order, there must be One who designed the order. The beauty of creation shows us that there is a powerful God who designed such beauty by His wisdom. Our God is infinitely greater than we could ever imagine. He is the Creator of all things – the galaxies, the planets, and all life. He is the One who created everything from nothing.

CHEW ON THIS: God called out to Samuel when he was 12 years old. He called Jeremiah to be national prophet when he was still a teenager. This is proof that God desires to be known and to be intimate with young people. He is available to everyone who desires to know Him. The question to consider: Do you want to know Him personally?

ACTION: Recognize that God is real, and He is not a man. It is natural and tempting to approach God as if He were a man. This is the reason why it is difficult for many people to relate with what the Bible says about the wonders and the greatness of God. The Bible clearly says God is not a man. He is not limited in the ways that humans are limited. He can do all things because He created everything by His infinite power and wisdom. This is not a mere religious cliché but an eternal truth. We must understand His nature so we can relate with Him as we should.

LESSON 43
GOD THE ETERNAL CREATOR (Part 1)

CONCLUSION

God is the Creator of all things. He created all things to display His glory. His majestic might is displayed in creation unto creation; Ps. 19:1-2. Creation exists to testify of and bear evidence of the gloriousness of God; Romans 1:20-21. Creation exists to bring praise to God; Ps. 148:1-4. This means the primary reason every human was created is to know and serve the Creator.

CLOSE IN PRAYER!!

WEEKLY QUIET TIME

DAY	BIBLE PASSAGE	SHARE YOUR DISCOVERIES BELOW
Monday	Psalm 19:1-4	
Tuesday	Psalm 40:1-5	
Wednesday	Psalm 40:12-17	
Thursday	Isaiah 6:1-3	
Friday	Rev. 4: 3-11	
Saturday	Daniel 7:9-10	

LESSON 44
GOD THE ETERNAL CREATOR (Part 2)

MAIN POINT: To know God is to know His character. Though creation reveals God's power and wisdom, there is a need to know that One with such power is good, trustworthy, and reliable. This is why God desires His children to know His character – the moral qualities that define His nature. It is God's desire to assure us that He can be trusted by revealing the perfection of His character to us in His word and by His Spirit.

BIBLE READING

Exodus 34:5-7

MEMORY VERSE

"Righteousness and justice are the foundation of Your throne; Mercy and truth go before Your face." Psalm 89:14.

INTRODUCTION
God created everything for His own pleasure. Everything exists because God created what pleased Him; Rev. 4:11. All things exist through and for Him; Col. 1:16. This means God made everything in heaven and on earth to reveal Himself. He wants us to know Who He is and to relate with Him personally and intimately.

CLASS DISCUSSION
- **What is His character?**
  - **Righteousness:** He exists in a state of moral perfection; 2 Chron. 12:6. He always acts in perfect accordance with His divine just standard. This is the outworking of God's holiness and purity. It also means God always does what is right by His divine justice code; Deut. 32:4.
  - **God is just:** God is perfectly upright in how He treats His creation; Ps. 89:14. He shows no partiality; Acts 10:34. He perfectly upholds, dispenses, and executes divine justice; Is. 30:18. He is just in giving reward and meting out punishment as required

LESSON 44
GOD THE ETERNAL CREATOR (Part 2)

by His justice system; Col. 3:25. He will never allow sin/evil to go unpunished; Ex. 34:7.

- **God is merciful and gracious:** God is eager to show compassion and forgiveness to His creation that are deserving of punishment and within His power to punish; Ex. 34:6; Deut. 4:31; Num. 14:18. He is slow to anger, long-suffering and abundantly patient; Ps. 145:8. He is kind and incredibly generous to His creation; James 1:5.
- **God is faithful:** He is perfectly steadfast in His allegiance and affection Lam. 3:22-23; 1 Cor. 1:9; Rev. 19:11. He perfectly adheres to His Word – Promises – and completely executes every duty He owes His creation; 1 Jn. 1:9. He never changes; Mal. 3:6. He never abandons or denies His promises and covenant; 2 Tim 2:13.
- **He is truthful and His Word is true:** There is no falsehood, lies or deception; Num. 23:19; Is. 45:19; Heb. 6:18. He is the One true God; Jer. 10:10. Jesus declared Himself the truth; Jn. 14:6. His Word is reliable and consistent with His character; 1 Jn. 5:20; Jn. 8:26. He can be trusted to keep His Word; Ps. 145:13.
- **He gives generously:** God takes pleasure in giving; Ps. 145:9; Rom. 5:8. He dispenses His fatherly role by generously providing for the needs of all creation, especially for His children; Luke 11:13; Jn. 3:16. He makes provisions for His children before they know to ask; Is. 65:22-24. He has given all things needed for life and godliness; 2 Pet. 1:3.

God is our perfect example in character. He is not only awesome in nature and capability, but also in character. He is perfect in character as He is in nature. His perfect character shows us the kind of character we ought to display if we identify as His children. The joy of being His children comes with the responsibility of displaying Christ-like character; Matt. 5:48.

CHEW ON THIS: God is immutable. This means He is constant in His character. His moral quality is forever constant. This means His motive and intentions are always aligned to His character. Everything He does

LESSON 44
GOD THE ETERNAL CREATOR (Part 2)

aligns with His character. This means knowing His character helps us understand His ways and His actions in our lives and in the world.

ACTION: Recognize Him as God over your life personally. While it is important to know He is God, it is much more important to acknowledge Him as God over our individual lives. Recognize that His God status means that there are severe consequences for ignoring or despising Him. We are created for His pleasure and our lives are to be lived out to fulfill His desire for which He created us. We must remember that though He is good and merciful, He is also the Judge of all the earth who will reward everyone for how they live their lives.

CONCLUSION

God is perfect in nature and character. He is forever merciful and faithful. His actions are always consistent with His words. He is worthy of honor and glory because His character and nature are perfect and eternal. He has revealed Himself through His word to help us know Him and give us the perfect example of who we are created to be. Remember, you are created in His image and likeness.

WEEKLY QUIET TIME

DAY	BIBLE PASSAGE	SHARE YOUR DISCOVERIES BELOW
Monday	Numbers 23:19	
Tuesday	Psalm 145:17	
Wednesday	Isaiah 40: 28-31	
Thursday	1 John 1:5-9	
Friday	Phil. 2: 1-4	
Saturday	Phil. 2: 5-11	

LESSON 45
REVIEW 4

TAKE A STEP BACK & REWIND

It is time to review the lessons 39 – 44.
- Ask your teacher about the TOPICS you don't understand.
- Be ready to participate and answer the questions for discussion.

CLASS DISCUSSION
- What would you say to a friend who wants to know about your Christian faith?
- Can you explain the TOPIC that challenges you the most?
- What did you learn from the previous lesson?
- Name two TOPICs from the previous lessons.
- Please share the most significant change you've experienced based on previous chapters.
- Feel free to ask questions for more clarity on any of the previous lessons.

WEEKLY QUIET TIME

DAY	BIBLE PASSAGE	SHARE YOUR DISCOVERIES BELOW
Monday	Psalm 5:1-2	
Tuesday	Psalm 5:7-8	
Wednesday	Psalm 73:1-14	
Thursday	Psalm 73:15-20	
Friday	Psalm 73:21-26	
Saturday	Psalm 73: 27-28	

LESSON 46
LIVING IN A CORRUPT AND UNFAIR WORLD

 MAIN POINT: Getting wisdom from the Psalms!

BIBLE READING
Psalm 73: 1-17

MEMORY VERSE
Text missing

INTRODUCTION
In Psalm 73, a man named Asaph expresses a frustration that many have shared. He was a faithful follower of God. In fact, he was a worship leader. But despite his efforts to serve and honor God, his life was marked by difficulty. In addition, as he looked around, he saw those who had no regard for God living in prosperity and apparent happiness.

CLASS DISCUSSION
Read Psalm 73
- Why did the psalmist open with "God is good"?
- What was his frustration?
- What happens when we envy and misunderstand the world?
- Explain the closing and conclusion of the psalmist in verse 27-28
- Is it vain to serve God?
- Read Psalm 14:1-7; what does this psalm mean to you?
- What do both Psalms (73 & 14) have in common?
- Think about your day-to-day faith; is your desire to follow and obey God's word being affected by your view of the people around you?

ACTION: Psalm 73:17-20; think about these verses by rewriting them in your own words:

_____
_____
_____

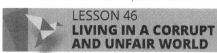

LESSON 46
LIVING IN A CORRUPT AND UNFAIR WORLD

CLOSE IN PRAYER!!

CONCLUSION

Wisdom psalms constitute one of the more distinctive kinds of palms in the Psalter. These are: 1, 14, 37, 73, 91, 112, 119, and 128. They are psalms that reflect on wisdom, on the fate of the righteous and the wicked, and on the Law.

WEEKLY QUIET TIME

DAY	BIBLE PASSAGE	SHARE YOUR DISCOVERIES BELOW
Monday	Acts 4:30-31	
Tuesday	Jeremiah 30:17	
Wednesday	Isaiah 38:16-17	
Thursday	Isaiah 40:29	
Friday	Psalm 34: 1-10	
Saturday	Psalm 34: 11-22	

LESSON 47
TOUGH QUESTIONS (Part 1)

 MAIN POINT: Choices are life-changing.

BIBLE READING

Genesis 13:5-18

INTRODUCTION
Life is all about choices and we need to get a better understanding of the truth to make the right choice.

MEMORY VERSE

"Give me understanding, so that I may keep your law and obey it with all my heart" Psalm 119:34

CLASS DISCUSSION
Note to teachers: Please help create an atmosphere where they can feel free to express their thoughts.
- o Use these discussion questions to help us all make the right decisions when faced with any of this life issues. Make sure you allow for everyone's input.
- o Do not rebuke the youths' responses. Leaders should facilitate the discussion so that other youth can defend the "right" answers.

Please support your responses with Scriptures where necessary and its okay to ask your teachers/leaders:
- Do you believe it's acceptable to watch R-rated movies? Why or why not?
- Do all religions lead to same way? Yes/No
- Do you believe parents should restrict their children from certain websites or give them total freedom on the World Wide Web?
- Do you believe there's music that Christians shouldn't listen to? If so, what music? Are there any TV shows that they shouldn't watch? If so, what shows?
- How would you define racism? Do you believe it's still a problem today?

LESSON 47
TOUGH QUESTIONS (Part 1)

- Can racism be only white to black? Can it be black to white? Can it exist beyond that with other races? Give some examples.
- How do you feel about different religions mixed marriages? How do you believe God views them?

CHEW ON THIS: Sometimes people make unwise choices which aren't momentous in themselves, but they lead to tragedies: A teenager chooses to ride with a friend who has been drinking, resulting in a serious accident and the loss of life. A girl decides to have a drink at a party, resulting in her letting down her inhibitions. She ends up pregnant or with a venereal disease. Since seemingly small decisions can have such momentous consequences, how can we protect ourselves from making wrong choices?

CLOSE IN PRAYER!!

ACTION: Always make choices that value fellowship with God over the approval of your friends and the world.

CONCLUSION
"The Purpose-Driven Life" begins the first chapter of his book with these words: "It's not about you. The purpose of your life is far greater than your own personal fulfillment, your peace of mind, or even your wildest dreams & ambitions. Focusing on ourselves will never reveal our life's purpose.

WEEKLY QUIET TIME

DAY	BIBLE PASSAGE	SHARE YOUR DISCOVERIES BELOW
Monday	James 1:14-15	
Tuesday	Proverbs 6:25	
Wednesday	Psalm 119:11	
Thursday	Psalm 4:4	
Friday	Psalm 37:31	
Saturday	Jeremiah 1:4-5	

LESSON 48
TOUGH QUESTIONS (Part 2)

 MAIN POINT: We must choose in line with God's principles.

BIBLE READING

Joshua 24:15

INTRODUCTION
Life is filled with choices. From the moment we wake up to the moment we go to bed at night our day is filled with choices. In fact, some sources suggest adults make 35,000 choices per day.

MEMORY VERSE

"I have hidden your word in my heart that I might not sin against you." Psalm 119:11

CLASS DISCUSSION
Note to teachers: Please help create an atmosphere where they can feel free to express their thoughts.
- Use these discussion questions to help us all make the right decisions when faced with any of this life issues. Make sure you allow for everyone's input.
- Do not rebuke the youths' responses. Leaders should facilitate the discussion so that other youth can defend the "right" answers.

Please support your responses with Scriptures where necessary and its okay to ask your teachers/leaders:
- Do you believe it's okay for Christians to have guns in their homes? Why or why not?
- Self-Injury Is Increasing in Teenagers: What can Parents do?
- Is it wrong for Christians to overeat? Why or why not?
- Is it okay for Christians to drink if they're of age? Why or why not?
- When – if ever – do you believe it's wrong for Christians to drink?

LESSON 48
TOUGH QUESTIONS (Part 2)

- Is it acceptable for Christians to smoke? Why or why not?
- Should Christians support the death penalty? If so, under what circumstances?
- Do you believe it's okay for a Christian to use weed – Cannabis?
- Is abortion ever okay? If so, when?

CHEW ON THIS: One of the most important decisions we will make has to do with who we will make our friend. "Do not be deceived: Evil company corrupts good habits" 1 Corinthians 15:33. The influence of a friend can rub off on us if we're not careful. That's why it's incredibly important to choose friends wisely.

ACTION: In every important decision, spend extra time in prayer and lean heavily upon the Lord. Take time to sit and talk with wise and godly individuals to hear what they have to say on the subject.

CLOSE IN PRAYER!

CONCLUSION: May God help us daily to make the best and right choices.

WEEKLY QUIET TIME

DAY	BIBLE PASSAGE	SHARE YOUR DISCOVERIES BELOW
Monday	Proverbs 12:26	
Tuesday	Proverbs 22:24- 25	
Wednesday	1 Corinthians 15:33	
Thursday	Galatians 6:7	
Friday	Job 12:10-11	
Saturday	Job 12:12-13	

LESSON 49
JESUS CALMS THE STORM

 MAIN POINT: If we want to live, grow, and persevere in faith, then it must be nourished with the word of God.

INTRODUCTION
The world this day is troubled with terrible circumstances that threaten human existence. Our community – including schools – is dominated with fear, famine of the word of God, fight to attain the top position, fire, and fury toward one another. Everyone on a daily occurrence must either flow with the storm or be still in the Word.

CLASS DISCUSSION
Read Matthew 8: 23-27 (Jesus Claiming the storm)
- What does this story teach about faith?
- What is the equivalent of a storm in modern day?
- Can storm be part of God's plan for your growth and development in Him?
- Do you believe that Jesus is there in the storm with you?
- Can you recall any challenging situation you had to deal with in the past?
- How did you come out of the situation?
- What would you have done better?
- Who gave you remarkable assistance?
- Where is our focus when we find ourselves in a difficult situation? On the problem or on God?

CHEW ON THIS: This story is a perfect illustration of being suddenly caught at the mercy of trying, or difficult, or even dangerous circumstances – circumstances in which we are helpless to do

BIBLE READING

Act 12: 1-8

MEMORY VERSE

"This is my command— be strong and courageous! Do not be afraid or discouraged. For the Lord your God is with you wherever you go." Joshua 1:9

LESSON 49
JESUS CALMS THE STORM

anything but cry out to God. Don't be surprised by the fact that, even when you follow Jesus faithfully, you still suddenly find yourself in the midst of a storm.

ACTION: Learn a Scripture that will help you to keep trusting God in difficult times. Don't be silent and stuff it in; but pray! Tell Jesus what concerns you.

Here are few Scriptures (tools) that will be helpful during a storm, write down the key "tool" used in each verse:

Acts 12:5 _____

Matthew 8:26 _____

Act 16:25_____

I Samuel 30:6 _____

CONCLUSION

If you are not a child of God, you will be sunk when the storm arose. But you can call on the Lord to save you now. Most assuredly, you would be able to experience calmness when the storm of life arises against you. Be strong and of good courage because the future is bright no matter the storm. Cheer up!

CLOSE IN PRAYER!!

WEEKLY QUIET TIME

DAY	BIBLE PASSAGE	SHARE YOUR DISCOVERIES BELOW
Monday	Joshua 1:9	
Tuesday	Romans 8:18	
Wednesday	Luke 1:35-37	
Thursday	Ezekiel 37:1-6	
Friday	Ezekiel 37:7-14	
Saturday	Joshua 1:5	

LESSON 50
BECKY'S CONVERSION STORY

 MAIN POINT: There is something to learn from each other's unique conversion story, today we learn from Becky's story.

BIBLE READING

Acts 9:1-10

INTRODUCTION
Rebekah (Becky) Cauchi is a serious follower of Jesus Christ; she's 21 years old. She lives and attends university in United Kingdom (Arts University, Bournemouth)

CLASS DISCUSSION
Read Becky's conversion interview story and discuss as a group. If you were asked these questions what will be your response? The youths should take turns answering these questions.

MEMORY VERSE

"Salvation is found in no one else, for there is no other name under heaven given to mankind by which we must be saved." Acts 4:12

Extract from Becky's conversion story!
Question: Tell us the story of your conversion to Jesus Christ. What exactly happened? And whom did God use?

Response: I wasn't always a passionate, born-again believer. In fact, it wasn't until I started university that I fully surrendered and began seeking the Lord wholeheartedly.

Like some, I had the privilege of a Christian upbringing; however, as my parents drifted from the church and the faith, I too forgot about the Jesus of my childhood. I became a lost and broken soul. My worldly, selfish, and angry attitude fueled by the trauma of a divided family caused me to lose sight of the Lord Jesus altogether.

LESSON 50
BECKY'S CONVERSION STORY

However, being the stubborn-minded and extremely deceived person I was, I would all the while proudly profess the faith of a good Christian girl. I was a fraud of a Christian. Only God knows how much of a mockery my life was against His name.

Fast forward to the end of an unhealthy relationship, job, and environment, I could hardly recognize myself. It was in this pit that I put my life before my eyes in deep assessment, and I came to realize that I was at a crossroad. One side leading further into my popular girl, wild living life of sin, and the other being a genuine pursuit of God.

This was where I chose God. As an unenthusiastic, poor reader, I persistently prayed for a hunger to read the Bible. Of course, the Lord answered me as I fell head over heels for His Word. I surrendered my life to Him fully.

Question: You actively preach the gospel. Tell us how that happened and where you preach and what usually happens when you do.

Response: Yes, I actively share the gospel street preaching. Being a natural evangelist, within the first year of my conversion, I found myself on the streets sharing the good news of Jesus with the public.

God divinely led me to other mission-minded evangelists who regularly went street preach together as a team. However, I was first exposed to gospel preaching though none other than a YouTube video.

It was a well-known American preacher called Ray Comfort, who documents and teaches simple evangelistic methods online via his YouTube account. After stumbling across one of his videos, I was so powerfully marked that I set my heart on doing it myself as soon as possible. Within the next week the Spirit led me to a niche group of evangelists in my area. That is where it all started for me.

LESSON 50
BECKY'S CONVERSION STORY

My God-given heart for people and bold convictions through the Word of God are continually fueling my service within this particular ministry. When preaching I get a mixture of reactions. In fulfilment of Scripture, hearts are always pierced, with some responding in anger, others responding with a humble plea for salvation in prayer afterwards.

Thanks for taking the time to share all of this with us, Becky.

ACTION: Recommit to praying for unsaved friends and loved ones. Want to share your story with us? Send it to us at <u>rccgnayouth1@gmail.com</u>! Take time to finish reading Becky's story *(Should Christians go to nightclubs (clubbing)?)*

CLOSE IN PRAYER!

WEEKLY QUIET TIME

DAY	BIBLE PASSAGE	SHARE YOUR DISCOVERIES BELOW
Monday	Matthew 1:21	
Tuesday	Acts 10:43	
Wednesday	Acts 13:26	
Thursday	1 Timothy 2:5	
Friday	Isaiah 9:6-9	
Saturday	Isaiah 9:10-15	

SHOULD CHRISTIANS GO TO NIGHTCLUBS (CLUBBING)?

Should Christians go to nightclubs (clubbing)?
Becky, tell us about yourself – where you grew up, your age, where and what you are currently studying: I grew up and have always lived by the South Coast of England. Now at the age of 21 years old, I am coming to the end of a three-year university degree course in Model Making. (Note: Model Making is the act of producing real 3D representations of buildings or objects.)

From your own experience and guidance of the Holy Spirit, what would you say to young Christian women and men about attending nightclubs and bars?

Clubbing is something I can confidently speak about because my old lifestyle would feed on such environments. The club was my playing field; it plats formed the pinnacle of the social ladder in which my empty identity was based on.

Before I gave my life to the Lord Jesus, I was inwardly broken and lost. I'd pull through an endless cycle of depressed weekdays at the excitement of a messy night out on Friday. These messy weekends were dark and dirty, but they were all the happiness and relief I knew, so in all honesty they were what I lived for.

SHOULD CHRISTIANS GO TO NIGHTCLUBS (CLUBBING)?

Lost, dead souls that are bound by addiction and deception gather in places such as the club because there it is socially acceptable and socially encouraged to act sinfully. I was once one of those souls. Now that Christ has saved me and given me His new life, I am entirely baffled at the idea of going back to that place of hopelessness for entertainment.

Ultimately, I believe the question is not whether going clubbing is a sin, but rather, will it draw us closer to God and bring Him honor? It's the motive behind it which is the stemming issue.

Therefore, if one gives the time to honestly assess the clubbing culture, I believe this question is self-explanatory. Ephesians 4 is my jumping base for this TOPIC:

You were taught, with regard to your former way of life, to put off your old self, which is being corrupted by its deceitful desires; to be made new in the attitude of your minds; and to put on the new self, created to be like God in true righteousness and holiness. (**Ephesians 4:22-24**)

One may argue that there are levels of personal convictions, but regardless of conviction, does participation aid our representation of Christ and would we honestly be comfortable clubbing in His presence? A classic night out is a group activity that always includes nonbelievers who will be actively committing sins before God. It's a certainty that this situation will involve you blending in with the crowd.

Do not present your members to sin as instruments for unrighteousness, but present yourselves to God as those who have been brought from death to life, and your members to God as instruments for righteousness. (Romans 6:13)

I long to be an available tool for righteousness. I don't want to blend into this world or be entertained by the things of this world. Does the flesh have any fellowship with the Spirit, or do they not oppose each other?

SHOULD CHRISTIANS GO TO NIGHTCLUBS (CLUBBING)?

As an ex-clubber I can safely say that the club is a meat market. Quite literally a feast of the flesh. The exercise of extensive alcohol, drugs and common fashion trends result in lust, drunkenness and zero sobrieties.

My own story of grace was a journey. The Lord had brought me from death to life; however, it took months before I got out of the club and party scene.

Personally, lust is a huge part of the reasoning as to why I strongly disagree with the notion that Christians should go clubbing.
Much of the music of this world opposes the virtues of the Spirit. Often explicitly sexual or violent. Their seductive tones entice the mind onto the same TOPICS and behaviors. Christians understand the power words can have.

I believe it is important to address personal motivations behind going clubbing. If I was honest with myself those years ago, I knew my selfish motives came from a place of darkness.

At the beginning of my conversion during an intense period of conviction, I found myself consciously blocking out most of the music I heard in the club, because deep down it was beginning to repulse and grieve me.

I remember going out in Manchester the year I gave my life to Jesus. I recall stepping back into the corner of the room as I had a cold realization that this was all delusional, counterfeit joy and light.
The club was utterly dark and all these people around me were blind. "What on earth am I doing here?" I remember asking myself. The Holy Spirit was convicting me and it wasn't a pleasant feeling. I didn't need to have someone tell me that what I was doing was wrong.

At that time in my life, the 'hard core' Christians I knew would confuse me greatly!

SHOULD CHRISTIANS GO TO NIGHTCLUBS (CLUBBING)?

I couldn't figure out what they had that I didn't, so all I could do was write them off as boring. How were they content without a drink in their hand? How did they not need to feed off the attention of the other sex? No wonder the club was the last place I'd find them.

In whom the god of this world hath blinded the minds of them which believe not, lest the light of the glorious gospel of Christ, who is the image of God, should shine unto them. (2 Corinthians 4:4)

On the other hand, evangelistically speaking, I might consider the club a platform to share the gospel; however, the overbearing volume of music and lack of sobriety makes this nearly impossible.

However, as evangelism requires social communication, the bar and smoking areas are potentially perfect for one-on-one conversations where seeds can be sown into ready hearts.

To conclude, I hold to my conviction not to attend a night out again; however, I'm also aware that not everyone can base their opinions on the same experiences as mine. Used with Permission from https://frankviola.org/2023/01/19/clubbing/

LESSON 51
WORDS MATTER!

BIBLE READING

Matthew 12:34-37

MEMORY VERSE

"The tongue can bring death or life; those who love to talk will reap the consequences." Proverbs 18:21

MAIN POINT: Most of us realize to a certain extent that words matter, yet few of us truly understand their power.

INTRODUCTION

The Word says that it is wisdom for us to watch our words and that through watching our words; we can defuse anger, bring life and healing, and even guard our souls!

CLASS DISCUSSION

- Why Words matter in the Bible? Because Words represent the truth and God's power! Isaiah 55:11, John 6:63
- Why do our words matter? Our words matter because we choose words to convey our thoughts and feelings.
- Why are words so powerful?
- What difference do words make in our lives?
- Write the words that made a difference in your life?

_____
_____
_____
_____

- Write the words that you wish were never said to you. REPLACE IT WITH GOD'S WORD.

_____
_____
_____
_____

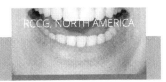

LESSON 51
WORDS MATTER!

- Think about a promise of God that has been fulfilled in your life, and are there promises that are yet to be fulfilled?

Write down the WORDS below and be determined to use them make a difference in your life and others.

1. Jeremiah 29:11; _____
   _____
   _____

2. Luke 1:37; _____
   _____
   _____

3. Romans 8:28; _____
   _____
   _____

4. Psalm 32: 8; _____
   _____
   _____

5. Isaiah 50:7; _____
   _____
   _____

6. Ephesian 1:19; _____
   _____
   _____

7. 6. Revelation 21:5 _____
   _____
   _____

CHEW ON THIS: The WORD says these things about what we speak:
- "Kind words are like honey – sweet to the soul and healthy for the body" Proverbs 16:24 (NLT)

LESSON 51
WORDS MATTER!

- "If you want to enjoy life and see many happy days, keep your tongue from speaking evil and your lips from telling lies" 1 Peter 3:10 (NLT)
- "Don't use foul or abusive language. Let everything you say be good and helpful, so that your words will be an encouragement to those who hear them." Ephesians 4:29 (NLT)
- "Too much talk leads to sin. Be sensible and keep your mouth shut." Proverbs 10:19
- "Gentle words are a tree of life; a deceitful tongue crushes the spirit." Proverbs 15:4 (NLT)
- "The heart of the godly thinks carefully before speaking; the mouth of the wicked overflows with evil words." Proverbs 15:28 (NLT)
- "It's not what goes into your mouth that defiles you; you are defiled by the words that come out of your mouth." Matthew 15:11 (NLT)
- "Watch your tongue and keep your mouth shut, and you will stay out of trouble." Proverbs 21:23

ACTION: Challenge yourself! Guard Your Mouth – Pray using this word: "Set a guard, O Lord, over my mouth; keep watch over the door of my lips." Psalm 141:3

CONCLUSION
Now, we can do much to guard our mouths and change the way we speak through practice and watchfulness. However, if we try to do this without seeking God's help, changing the way we speak can take much longer and be more challenging than it need be. Because with God, all things are possible, and we do not need to rely only upon our own strength!

CLOSE IN PRAYER

WEEKLY QUIET TIME

DAY	BIBLE PASSAGE	SHARE YOUR DISCOVERIES BELOW
Monday	John 1:1-3	
Tuesday	John 6:63-70	
Wednesday	2 Corinthians 3:6	
Thursday	John 6:68	
Friday	Psalm 24	
Saturday	Matthew 12:34-40	

BE CAREFUL WHO YOU ASSOCIATE WITH
(Heartbreaking story)

The identity of a 59-year-old man killed in Toronto after allegedly being "swarmed" by a group of eight teenage girls has been released by Canadian authorities.

Ken Lee was fatally stabbed on a cold night in mid-December.

Police said he was surrounded by girls aged between 13 and 16, who were arrested nearby and charged in the days after the attack. Lee had recently been living in a homeless shelter.

Toronto police released his identity on Tuesday, weeks after the 18 December attack which took place near midnight local time in the city's downtown core. Police have said they believe Lee may have been preyed upon because he was spotted carrying alcohol. He later died in hospital.

The girls are currently facing second-degree murder charges. As minors, they cannot be identified under Canadian law. *Police said the girls first met online before gathering in person the night of the attack, possibly for the first time. They do not believe it was gang related.*

BE CAREFUL WHO YOU ASSOCIATE WITH
(Heartbreaking story)

On Wednesday, police said they were looking for victims of a group of up to 10 girls who allegedly assaulted several people at public transit stations in the hours before the attack on Lee. Police did not say the attacks are connected to the fatal stabbing, but law enforcements sources told Canadian media that the girls are suspects in the assaults.

The attack on Lee shocked the city, with Toronto Mayor John Tory saying he was "deeply disturbed" by the case.

"I've been in policing for almost 35 years, and you think you've seen it all," Detective Sergeant Terry Browne told the Associated Press in a December interview. "If this isn't alarming and shocking to everyone, then we're all in trouble quite frankly."

Speaking to reporters after the assault, Detective Browne called the assault an "anomaly", adding that the girls arrived to the downtown Toronto area from different parts of the city. Three of the girls have had prior run-ins with police, authorities said. Lee's name was added on Tuesday to the Toronto Homeless Memorial, maintained by the Church of the Holy Trinity near the city centre.

Curried BBC News Story, Washington - By Brandon Drenon -
Read Proverbs 1:10-19

LESSON 52
TAKE A STAND

 MAIN POINT: Be resolute! Be determined and unwavering in your faith.

INTRODUCTION
Some people who call themselves Christians will not stand up for anything. They are so ruled by the fear of man that they are hiding their light under a bushel basket and hoping desperately that no one finds out they're a Christian.

CLASS DISCUSSION
Answer the following questions; please support your answers with the Scriptures.
- Should Christians celebrate Halloween?
- What does the Bible say about tattoos?
- Once saved always saved? / Can a Christian lose salvation?
- What does the Bible say about suicide? What about a believer who commits suicide?
- What happens after death?
- What does the Bible say about gambling? Is gambling a sin?
- What does the Bible say about sex before marriage?

ACTION: Make up your mind ahead of time; do not just follow others blindly, and be sure of the truth on how and when to take a stand.

CHEW ON IT: Are you standing for truth?

CLOSE IN PRAYER!!

VERY IMPORTANT: National Hopeline Network: 1-800-SUICIDE

BIBLE READING

Daniel 1:8-16

MEMORY VERSE

"Because whoever is ashamed of Me and of My teachings, of him will the Son of Man be ashamed when He comes in the [threefold] glory (the splendor and majesty) of Himself and of the Father and of the holy angels." Luke 9:46

LESSON 52
TAKE A STAND

USA National Suicide Prevention Lifeline: 988Suicide hotlines available in most countries: http://www.suicide.org/international-suicide-hotlines.html

📖 WEEKLY QUIET TIME

DAY	BIBLE PASSAGE	SHARE YOUR DISCOVERIES BELOW
Monday	James 4:13-17	
Tuesday	Jeremiah 29:11	
Wednesday	Philippians 1:6	
Thursday	James 1:5	
Friday	Proverbs 27:12	
Saturday	Philippians 4:6	

LESSON 53
FOURTH INTERACTIVE SESSION AND QUIZ 4

Dear Teachers,

Please note the following:
- Make the interactive session interesting.
- Ensure the teens participate by allowing them to contribute and state what they have learned as well as ask questions.
- Prepare your own questions and quizzes that you will ask them based on the previous lessons.
- You may give gifts to those who perform well in the quiz.
- Create an avenue for the teens to give useful suggestions on how the Sunday School Class can be improved.

Below are some suggested questions you can ask — feel free to add to them!
- Mention five or more previous lesson topics.
- Ask if they remember the Bible passages of each lesson.
- Ask them to recite the memory verses.
- Ask questions from the Activities session as well.
- Ask them questions on the body of the lessons.

WEEKLY QUIET TIME

DAY	BIBLE PASSAGE	SHARE YOUR DISCOVERIES BELOW
Monday	1 Corinthians 2:1-5	
Tuesday	1 Corinthians 2:6-12	
Wednesday	1 Corinthians 2:13-16	
Thursday	1 Corinthians 3:1-9	
Friday	1 Corinthians 3:10-17	
Saturday	1 Corinthians 3: 18-23	

Made in the USA
Middletown, DE
12 May 2023

30417376R00077